TRANSMONTANUS 9

Kokanee

Published by New Star Books

Series Editor: Terry Glavin

Other books in the Transmontanus series

Kokanee

THE REDFISH AND THE KOOTENAY BIOREGION

Don Gayton

TRANSMONTANUS / NEW STAR BOOKS VANCOUVER

This is a rededication to my wife, Judy Harris, and our children. They are my centre. Thanks to Harvey Andrusak, Ken Ashley, and Red Wassick for their generosity in sharing information; to Judy, for her many helpful comments on the manuscript; to Art Stock, for his photographic expertise; and to the Columbia Basin Trust / Royal British Columbia Museum for financial support. Lastly, thanks to Terry Glavin, Rolf Maurer, and the staff at New Star for their commitment to this book.

Contents

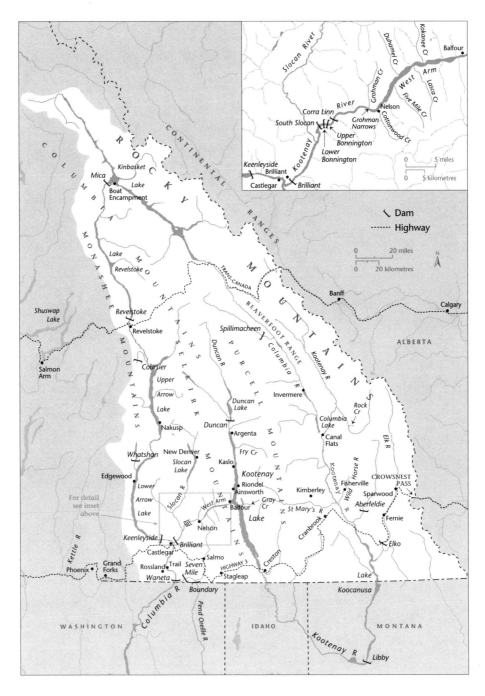

The Kootenays today. Inset: The Kokanee River between Nelson and Castlegar — the place where the story of the kokanee begins.

Three generations of Gaytons: the author, Don Gayton III; his father, Don, Sr.; and son, Ivan Gayton, in 1991. GAYTON FAMILY PHOTO

Tangle

My ageing father sat in a lawn chair on the Nelson city wharf, baitcasting, while I used his father's bamboo fly rod, a family heirloom made of Tonkin cane. Even though he had a career as an engineer, Dad defined himself as a salmon and steelhead fisherman. His hip-waders would hang in the hall closet, and you could always find bait smelt in the freezer. Many of the moves our family made when I was growing up were not done for occupational reasons, but in search of better fishing grounds. In each new place, I would learn the names of the local rivers before I learned my address. There was the Stillaguamish and the Dungeness, the Trinity and the Humptulips. I got to know the fogbound salmon towns of Oregon and Washington — Moclips, Sekiu, and Tillamook — and I heard the stories of his trips to Prince Rupert and to Kodiak.

Dad and I hadn't fished together for years, but he was old and ill and wanted to go on one more nostalgic salmon expedition, maybe to Campbell River. When I quoted him the prices of fishing charters, his Depression-era sensibilities were offended. I think he also sensed my hesitation about a trip that would pit the current salmon situation against his memories of it from forty years previous. In the end, he came to my landlocked town of Nelson, British Columbia, and we fished for kokanee from the

city wharf, sandwiched unromantically between the hotel and
the airstrip.

We fished mostly in silence, both fully aware this was our last
trip together, both knowing our distant and sometimes stormy
father-son relationship was approaching endgame. Neither of us
fished with much conviction; Dad because he didn't know the
kokanee, and I because I didn't really expect to catch anything on
a dry fly from a city dock next to an airstrip. But the methodical
swish of cast lines and the click of reels was satisfying enough,
and the darkened planks of the dock began to heat up pleasantly
in the sun.

Dad's enduring frame of reference for sport fishing was catching big kings and chinooks up and down the West Coast in the
1950s and '60s. He knew something had gone terribly wrong with
those salmon runs, but wasn't sure what it was or who to blame,
and so retreated into a kind of aged silence. He, like many men,
fished from a curious combination of motivations: a passionate
attachment to nature, an enduring mystification about his role in
society, and a kind of primitive male satisfaction in showing that
he could still bring occasional food home from the wild. His rage
over the turning of the environmental leaf, from the unspoiled
abundance of his youth to the current climate of uncertainty, seasonal closures, and environmental disasters, was played out in
fishing. As I watched him cast and reel, I wondered over how
many Pacific rivers and coastlines he had performed that same
motion. The bright aluminium lawn chair I had brought for him
to sit on looked garishly out of place against the backdrop of water
and mountain.

I reminded Dad of the time he came home with the first steelhead he claimed to have caught. I was about ten then, and we
had moved to a rural area on Washington's Olympic Peninsula,
mainly for the quality of its steelhead waters. Dad fished unsuc-
cessfully for weeks and months for that legendary and elusive fish
until an accomplished local fisherman took pity and gave him
one. Dad brought it home triumphantly, claiming he had caught
it, but he was a lousy liar and my sister and I forced a confession
out of him. Dad and I had a good laugh about that, but he
reminded me that midway through his second winter of fishing
he finally did catch his first steelhead.

A sudden strong tug on my fly rod grabbed my attention and I realized that this symbolic fishing exercise had suddenly been hijacked by a real fish, and a feisty one at that. I had lots of slack line at my feet, so I paid some out, slowly, at the same time as I raised the rod high into the air. The ten feet of ancient Tonkin cane, which I often cursed in dense bush, came into its own, bending in modulated arcs as the fish worked frantically back and forth. Dad stopped his casting and watched, the approving professor beaming as his graduate performed. I offered him the rod as a gesture, but I knew he wouldn't take it. At that moment I would have given anything for the fish to have taken his hook instead of mine.

I would have given anything for the fish to have taken his hook instead of mine.

I knew I was going to keep this fish, so I played it slowly, letting the runs and years and contradictions spin backward and forward between us. At the appropriate moment Dad came around behind me and in a movement surprisingly graceful for his age and bulk, he bent down and netted the fish, tail first. It was a sleek, platinum-sided kokanee, an obvious salmonid, bearing all the classic characteristics of Dad's storied kings and chinooks, except for the size. It was about fifteen inches long, a healthy length for a mature kokanee, but smaller than its coastal doppelganger, the sockeye. We both marvelled at the fish's clean, sculpted lines, its perfect marriage between streamlining and muscle.

Here was a tangle, one far more complex than any mess I have been able to make with six-pound test: a tangle of fathers and ecology, engineering and fish, regions and people. Dad was part of that boundlessly energetic postwar generation for whom the re-shaping of the earth with technology was not only a right, but a sacred duty. But his was a generation that also loved the outdoors, and the manly arts of hunting and fishing. The irony was that this man, this salmon-lover, exercised his talents precisely in those technological earthworks that so negatively affected the life of every fish in North America, especially the salmonids. As an eager young high-school kid, Dad spent an enthralled summer as a labourer on the Grand Coulee dam project, that giant stake driven through the heart of the world's greatest salmon river. It was not surprising that he went on to become an engineer. Berms and penstocks, cantilevers and caissons: fitting these to the earth was seen as the western male mandate, which he passionately embraced. I don't hold him to blame though; he was a true scion of his own era, as am I of my more ambiguous one.

He held the kokanee for quite a while, looking at every graceful detail. This was a fish that had also suffered from technological modifications of its environment, although the burnished silver of this one gave no hint. Then Dad finally handed them back to me, the fish, the engineering, the generations, the tangle; American coastal father offering silent approval to renegade Canadian Interior son. I slipped the kokanee into a plastic bag, wishing that I hadn't lost the old wicker creel that was companion to Grandfather's cane fly rod, and our last fishing trip was over.

We both felt the curious power in this wild creature, beyond the essential marvel of its separate life form so different from ours, and beyond the power of its undeniable beauty. When we as passionate observers, thoughtful fishers, or scientists are able to experience their presence deeply, then we recognize these wild animals and plants do carry the power of symbol. The opportunity to sense wild things in this way, and thus to appreciate their symbolic power, is in decline. Transactions now are largely with machines and each other, not with nature. And in our modern, science-based society, we have convinced ourselves that we cannot tolerate symbolic representations.

Humans do not have dominion over beasts of the field and fishes of the sea, that much I believe.

Humans do not have dominion over beasts of the field and fishes of the sea, that much I believe. On the other hand, I don't revere nature over humanity. I do believe that organisms and ecosystems, like that silver-sided kokanee, have an inherent right to existence. Perhaps that is what separates my father's experience from mine. He lived in an age when the average person did not have to take a position on the value of nature or judge whether society's actions were destructive to it. But now, as undeniable evidence links us to species extinctions and ecosystem degradation, evidence my father suspected but never had to contend with, we must make those judgments. The grand experiment for us is whether we can grant and respect those multiple rights of nature's existence, a kind of ecological charter of rights, if you will. If we can somehow do that, then we will have the diverse regional parts of this big blue marble as a permanent stage on which to play out our mostly tawdry — but occasionally splendid — human dramas.

Wild things, and the regional ecologies that caress and support them, can tell us much, if we learn to listen. I think I hear the kokanee speaking of organism, of the far-reaching connectedness of ecology, and of a bioregional culture of the Kootenays.

Dead spawners, West Arm of Kootenay Lake. They are sampled for weight, size, age, and remaining eggs. PHOTO BY ART STOCK

Proglacial

There is a morning, back in time, when this region of British Columbia they call the Kootenays changed from ice and rock to land and water, from Pleistocene to Holocene. This morning can be described neatly in multiples of ten; at the beginning of the morning, some ten millennia ago, the glaciers lay across the landscape a thousand metres thick. At the end of the postglacial morning, a thousand years later, the continental glaciers were gone.

One of the very first inhabitants of the region, arriving literally on the meltwaters of receding glaciers, is a fish. This fish is an extravagant gift from the Pacific Ocean to the Interior. It is an elusive flash of molten silver, a lustful reproductive torrent of fire-engine red, a marvel of adaptation, an icon of regional culture, and a pawn of industry. Its name has cycled through various cultures as kukeni, redfish, kokanee, kickininee, silver, *Oncorhynchus nerka*. These cultures have depended on it, studied it, even brought it close to annihilation, but none has ever completely possessed it.

The story of our kokanee begins in the rockbound bed of the Kootenay River between the present-day communities of Nelson and Castlegar, where the entombed remains of a waterfall can be found. Now wrapped in the concrete embrace of the Corra Linn hydroelectric dam, Lower Bonnington Falls once represented the

Captain Palliser, best known for defining the drought-prone triangle of prairie in southern Alberta and Saskatchewan, also mapped extensively in British Columbia. The scope and reach of the 1857–1860 Palliser Expedition makes it the Canadian equivalent of the Lewis and Clark Expedition.

single largest drop in the 700-kilometre-long Kootenay River system. Early accounts of the falls, and of the smaller Upper Bonnington set just above it, are sketchy. Captain James Palliser's 1860 map has a notation "falls, 40 feet." The first hydroelectric dam, the predecessor to Corra Linn, was actually built on part of the falls in 1898, to supply electricity to the nearby mining communities of Rossland and Trail. The earliest known photograph of the falls was taken in 1902, after it was already partly harnessed. The picture shows foaming slabs of white water exploding — not downward, but straight out — from between jagged black rocks, and a cloud of spray hovers above the plunge pool. The falls looks like the single bastion that controlled the entire river.

Just downstream from Bonnington, a bizarre angular column of granite rises ten metres out of the water in the middle of the channel: Coyote Rock. The column's flat top, covered by scrub vegetation, suggests an original land surface, which means that at some point, massive quantities of rock around it were eroded and smashed away, leaving only this durable pillar. Its skin is craggy and fractured. Seams and fissures of distinct rock types run through it. Bonnington Falls was a natural barrier to spawning salmon and a mother to the kokanee. Coyote Rock, untouched by glaciers, floods, and dams, celebrates that capricious and wilful act of nature.

Contained within the massive forces of mountain geology, small but significant acts of biology can occur that permanently change the shape and meaning of a place. One such act was the formative moment of the kokanee, and it took place at the falls, amidst the chaos of the end of the last Ice Age.

The regional glaciers of the Wisconsinan, the last of our four Ice Ages, were continent-flattening behemoths. They sprawled across the landscape for millennia, burying valleys like the Kootenay, Columbia, and Okanagan under thousand-metre depths of ice, and extending well below the forty-ninth parallel into present-day northern Washington, Idaho, and Montana. What life there was in the Kootenays either lay dormant under the ice or clung precariously to unglaciated mountaintops. The sheer size and power of these glaciers put them in the same world-shaping league as the elemental forces of volcanoes and plate tectonics.

Even though the Wisconsinan lasted for some 30,000 years,

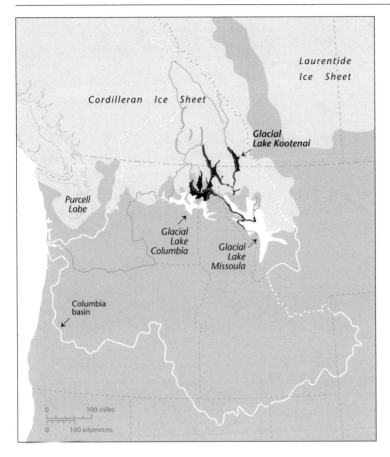

The Kootenays and the Columbia River basin 12,500 years ago — just the other day, in evolutionary terms.

its end came suddenly. At 12,500 BP (Before Present), the ice monsters still swelled and writhed; by 9500 BP there were only pathetic glacial remnants cowering on the north lees of high peaks. As the ice sheets retreated, huge volumes of water were released, and temporary waterbodies, known as proglacial lakes, formed right against the snout of the receding glaciers. A classic example of the melting glacier/proglacial lake complex was the mighty Purcell lobe, a southward extension of the Cordilleran Glacier that slid all the way down the Kootenay Valley to northern Idaho.

Extruded southward by the phenomenal weight of ice accumulated in the cleft that would become Kootenay Lake, the Purcell lobe grew and melted simultaneously. By plugging the sole outflow channel that would allow the brimming meltwaters to drain westward out of the Bitterroot Mountains to the Columbia

River and the ocean, the Purcell lobe created Glacial Lake Missoula. (Superlative adjectives become repetitive in describing this era, so Lake Missoula's volume can speak for itself: 700 *cubic miles* of water.) The Purcell lobe, rotted and weakened by the warming climate, finally broke loose, unleashing Lake Missoula's waters in a biblical-scale flood.

Retreating further back into Canada, the same Purcell lobe created a second temporary lake, Glacial Lake Kutenai, a seminal event in the life of the kokanee. This regional lake spread east and west, filling and connecting the river valleys and inundating present-day Kootenay Lake, the West Arm, and Bonnington Falls. There is even speculation that Lake Kutenai lapped up against the Rockies for a time.

Into this temporary lake swam the far-ranging and ever-willing sockeye salmon, en route from the Pacific Ocean, pursuing its particular anadromous habit of spawning in streams that flow into freshwater lakes with outlets to the ocean. Several other fish came with the sockeye, including the mountain whitefish and the Yellowstone cutthroat trout. In their upstream journey, they passed unwittingly over the drowned and quiescent rocks of Bonnington Falls. They may also have arrived by swimming up the Pend Oreille drainage and accessing the Kootenay watershed over a low drainage divide between Sandpoint and Bonners Ferry, Idaho. The sockeye and its saltwater compatriots quickly established spawning areas in the streams flowing into Glacial Lake Kutenai, and along the shores of the lake itself.

Several other fish came with the sockeye, including the mountain whitefish and the Yellowstone cutthroat trout.

By 9500 BP, though, the meltwaters had drained away to present proportions and Glacial Lake Kutenai was no more. The tortured granite of Coyote Rock and Upper and Lower Bonnington Falls reappeared. This complex became the rocky valve that controlled the entire Kootenay river and lake system, as well as the movement of fish.

The reappearance of Bonnington spelled a permanent end to sockeye spawning in Kootenay Lake. Every fish species has an upstream "burst speed," a rate of maximum swimming energy output it can maintain for no more than a few seconds before rest is required. Newly re-established Bonnington Falls' onrush of water far exceeded the burst speed abilities of even the athletic sockeye, and it became a permanent biological barrier. Aspiring sockeye spawners were forced to turn back from the Bonnington spigot, and young Kootenay Lake sockeye, perhaps sensing an irrevocable and fatal quickening of the waters just above the falls, chose to stay put, giving up forever their anadromous habit, so becoming kukenai, the redfish, *Oncorhynchus nerka*, the salmon of the mountains, the kokanee.

Columbia River sockeye and Kootenay Lake kokanee, although capable of mating and producing offspring, were now geographically unable to do so. Although the two fish still share the same gene pool, they are, in the language of genetics, "reproductively isolated." In order to survive, Kootenay Lake's kokanee made the necessary physiological adaptations to live, feed, and reproduce completely in fresh water.

Although Kootenay Lake/Bonnington Falls is the most famous example, there is abundant evidence that landslides, temporary ice dams, and even hydroelectric dams can also turn sockeye into kokanee. Just to prove their unpredictability though, kokanee do inhabit lakes that maintain passable ties to salt water. Shuswap Lake, which has viable connections to the ocean via the Thompson and the Fraser rivers, hosts both resident kokanee and spawning sockeye. This odd situation develops when residual sockeye, which can return to the ocean but simply choose not to, stay on in the lake to become voluntary kokanee.

The kokanee of Kootenay Lake are sometimes referred to as "the fish that can't go home," prevented by Bonnington from roaming the open stretches of the North Pacific Ocean, the true domain of the salmon. Modern theories of salmonid evolution have turned this notion on its ear, however. Current thinking is that the freshwater trout were the earliest salmonids, and the saltwater anadromous races, such as the sockeye, evolved from freshwater origins. So the kokanee is less a homeless wanderer than a prodigal son. Like the marine mammals, this creature began in one environment, adapted to a completely different one, and then returned to the original environment again.

The sockeye-kokanee duality is not unique; the prized ocean-going steelhead is actually just an adventurous rainbow trout. Other such freshwater and saltwater versions exist in the salmon world, and in every case the saltwater race grows to a larger final size than the freshwater one does, because of the greater food resources that the ocean provides.

The Columbia and the Fraser river systems are the centre of the freshwater phase of the sockeye's universe, but the runs of the Columbia and its main tributary, the Snake, have been devastated by dams. The Grand Coulee dam, built on the Columbia in the 1930s, virtually destroyed any sockeye and chinook runs above it. Not only did the dam create a physical barrier to passage, but the vast upstream impoundments it created did not favour spawning or fry survival. In a desperate attempt to re-establish dam-decimated sockeye runs on the upper Snake River in Idaho, local kokanee fry are being transported downstream to see if they will revert back to sea-run sockeye, thus preserving the genetics of the run. Chances appear slim though, since these fish still have to negotiate a dozen dams and a dozen stagnant reservoir impoundments to get back to the upper reaches of the Snake to spawn, and then their vulnerable offspring have to run the same gauntlet in reverse.

The closing of this scientific creation story comes as newly minted kokanee, still fresh from the Bonnington Falls trauma that separated them from the parent sockeye, began to explore the waters of Kootenay Lake, their new home. Slowly, they learned the complex geography and waters of the lake basin, finding favoured places and staking out spawning gravels. Feeding, and being fed upon, they became the pioneer builders of the Kootenay Lake food chain. Like their brethren the sockeye, the kokanee would be affected by dams, but that was still far in the future. First they would have a few millennia to explore the new stability of the Holocene, coming to terms with this unknown lake and its unfolding ecology.

Kootenay Lake looking south from near Kaslo. An average depth of 100 metres contributes to the scarcity of nutrients in the lake. PHOTO BY ART STOCK

Mountains and Rivers

L ife in the Kootenays — for both fish and people — is played
out on a stage consisting of two rivers and four mountain
ranges. The Kootenay region of B.C. is a crude triangle, bounded
by the Rockies on the east, the Monashee range (which divides
the Kootenays from the Okanagan) to the west, and the U.S. border to the south. In between the Rockies and the Monashees lie
the Purcell and the Selkirk ranges, collectively known as the
Columbia Mountains. The trend of these four ranges is roughly
northwestward. Our two rivers, the Kootenay and the Columbia,
wander through these mountain ranges, sometimes following
their lead, sometimes not. Even in this modern era that demands
we either overcome geography or ignore it, these mountains and
rivers still dominate.

The Kootenay forms part of the massive Columbia River
watershed. The outline of the Columbia's drainage basin traces a
tortuous path across the geology, history, and politics of western
North America. The U.S. portion of the watershed includes all of
Idaho, most of Washington and Oregon, western Montana, and
even small chunks of California, Nevada, Utah, and Wyoming.
On the Canadian side, the central part of the basin is triangular
with the forty-ninth parallel as the bottom. The right-hand side of
the basin triangle follows the Alberta border almost up to the Yel-
lowhead Highway, which runs between Jasper and Prince
George. The left-hand side of the triangle wanders southward

again, but then takes a wide westward swing to include the Kettle, Okanagan, and Similkameen river valleys.

Secondary roads crisscross the Kootenay landscape, following the major drainages. Logging roads run everywhere, but nearly all of them dead-end high up in tributary valleys. The Trans-Canada Highway just grazes the northern tip of the Kootenays at Revelstoke. The one complete east-west route through the region, Highway Three, follows a circuitous path from the Crowsnest Pass through Cranbrook, Castlegar, and Grand Forks, closely tracking the route of Edgar Dewdney's original westward trail. Between Creston and Salmo the highway crosses the Stagleap, the highest pass in Canada that is open year-round. In winter, maintenance workers close the pass periodically and trigger avalanches on the open and risky snowslopes above the highway. West of Castlegar lie Grand Forks and the Boundary country, hydrologically part of the Columbia basin (the Kettle River flows into the Columbia), but culturally separate from the Kootenays.

In satellite images, the landforms of the Kootenays look surprisingly like the reticulate surface of the brain. This prodigious mountain complexity creates a wide variety of habitats over continuously varying aspect, elevation, soil, and bedrock type, at the same time as it makes a hash of road trips. The small community of Argenta, at the north end of Kootenay Lake, is only 75 kilometres as the crow flies from the East Kootenay community of Invermere. But the terrain that separates them is a rugged and unroaded section of the Purcell range, so to drive from one town to the other takes a ferry ride and the best part of a day.

The Kootenay River, the main water source of Kootenay Lake, is a classic Rocky Mountain river, originating at the foot of Castle Mountain, in the B.C. Rockies northwest of Banff. Moving down between the Continental and Beaverfoot ranges, it finally breaks westward out of the maze of mountains and enters the broad, flat valley of the Rocky Mountain Trench. The twin ramparts of Mount Grainger and Mount Sabine mark this braided and youthful stream's exit point from the Rockies. Once into the Trench, the river promptly curls southward again, heading downvalley, toward Montana.

Two kilometres north of the river's curl, on the other side of a log yard, beyond the small community of Canal Flats in some low-lying ground that trends from scrub forest to willow hummock to coarse mats of bulrush, lies Columbia Lake, the source of the north-flowing Columbia River. Hidden somewhere in the boggy ground in between, or perhaps even in the log yard itself, is a crucial drainage divide, a faint bevel to the landscape, that separates the Columbia and the Kootenay, their biology, and their history. From this divide at Canal Flats they flee in opposite directions, the Columbia to the north, the Kootenay south, each hugging the west slope of the Rockies, and each responding to that small but significant difference of slope and gravity at Canal Flats.

> *The Kootenay's broad and mazy delta as it enters the lake is a biological treasure, filled with migratory waterbirds.*

Shortly after it passes Cranbrook, the Kootenay begins to slow down as it reacts to the effect of Libby dam, far downstream in Montana. After it is released from the stagnant waters behind Libby, the river swings abruptly northward again. Geologists theorize the Kootenay continued southward prior to the Miocene, but the great lava flows of that epoch forced it to double back on itself. The river re-enters British Columbia at Creston, spilling into the hundred-kilometre-long, five-kilometre-wide fissure that is Kootenay Lake, legacy of an ancient geological fault. The Kootenay's broad and mazy delta as it enters the lake is a biological treasure, filled with migratory waterbirds.

The Kootenay River fills the lake from the south end, aided by the smaller Duncan River that empties into its north end, and the dozen or so creeks scattered in between. At the lake's outflow point, known as the West Arm, the Kootenay becomes half river, half lake. At the chokepoint, Grohman Narrows, just below Nelson, it regains river status only momentarily before it absorbs the impact of four dams in a thirty-kilometre stretch. The Kootenay finally ends its lengthy separation from the Columbia and joins it at the Doukhobor community of Brilliant, near Castlegar. The reunion is not a passive one; they come straight at each other, each in its rockbound channel, and at the last minute both unite and turn southward, forming the arms of a Y. The newly swollen Columbia, having now received the waters of its second-largest tributary, becomes the base of the Y, then heads determinedly south and west, to Washington, Oregon, and eventually the Pacific.

It is curious how these two sister rivers start so close to each other and then fly off in exactly opposite tangents. Only when they are 500 kilometres apart — the Columbia at an isolated spot known as Boat Encampment and the Kootenay far down in western Montana — do they reconsider. Doubling back on themselves, each mirroring the other's direction, they finally join and acknowledge the westward pull of salt water.

Finding a river outlet to the Pacific Ocean was a passionate mission for explorers making the first stumbling explorations of the terra incognita west of the Canadian Rockies. West-flowing rivers populated their dreams, and one can imagine the consternation of men like David Thompson, after slogging their way across the snowbound Rockies, when they encountered major rivers flowing perversely southward (the Kootenay) and northward (the Columbia), *not westward*, as they wished. Both rivers were roundly cursed. For many years after its first discovery, explorers and cartographers had the Columbia River emptying into the Arctic Ocean.

When I was still a newcomer to the Kootenays, I was invited to attend a national ecological conference in Banff, Alberta. Conference organizers asked participants to bring a small jug of water from the waterbody nearest their homes. During the outdoor opening ceremony, each of us was supposed to describe the source of our water and then pour it onto the ground in a symbolic gesture. I dutifully went down to the Nelson city dock, put a small sample of the Kootenay's water in a plastic bottle, and took it with me on the long drive to Banff. During the conference I happened to casually examine a detailed map of the central Rockies and realized that the same Kootenay River arises less than a hundred kilometres from Banff. It was as if I knew less western geography than Thompson did two centuries earlier. But after getting over the embarrassment of having described the Kootenay as a far-off river, I began to feel a sense of connectedness; Banff and these glamorous Rockies were now partly mine, by right of common watershed.

David Thompson is a complex, tragic figure in the history of Canadian exploration. He finally reached the mouth of the Columbia River shortly after John Jacob Astor's party did, thus missing the opportunity to lay British claim to Washington and Oregon by a matter of a few weeks. Historians have blamed Thompson's obsession with accurate mapmaking, and his patient avoidance of any hostilities with First Nation groups, for the delay. In fact, Thompson was in the bush for so long that he was out of touch with events and had no idea he was in a race.

This, the earliest known photograph of Bonnington Falls, was taken in 1902 after the falls was already partly harnessed. CYRIL SWANNELL / BC ARCHIVES PHOTO I-33941

First People

Coyote tricked the people of the Dalles, on the lower Columbia River, and stole some of their magnificent salmon. He led the obedient salmon upstream, wandering along the great river and its tributaries. As he arrived at the various encampments, he would offer the people some of his fish in exchange for the opportunity to sleep with one of their women. Some groups agreed, and for them, Coyote released the salmon into their waters. Others did not agree to Coyote's terms. When Coyote encountered an obstinate group, he would fly into a towering rage and smash his walking stick against the riverbank, making a cliff in the riverbed so the local people upstream would never taste his salmon. Such was the case at Bonnington, where the Sinixt people refused to provide Coyote with one of their women. So angry was Coyote that he not only created the falls to stop the salmon, but he also left a crude reminder of his power, a kind of obscene gesture, in the form of Coyote Rock.

The full complexity of this Sinixt story is not mine to tell, but presenting its dry husk in a paragraph is enough to illustrate a point. The Coyote story is an alternate explanation, coming from a different language, culture, and worldview, for the denial of the sockeye and the creation of Kootenay Lake's kokanee. When told in its entirety, this story is a fine alternative to my story of proglacial lakes, burst speed, and reproductive isolation. The complete Coyote legend carries accumulated ecological and geographical insights of a First Nations people; mine carries those of the western scientific community. The Coyote story is an example of what academics refer to as indigenous peoples' knowledge (IPK). IPK is a vast body of knowledge generated from a worldview totally different from that of western science, but there is every reason to see these two worldviews and bodies of knowledge as equally important, equally valid.

The Sinixt (Lakes), Okanagan, and Ktunaxa peoples made use of the kokanee as part of a series of complex seasonal and elevational movements through the Kootenays to harvest fish, deer, mountain sheep, berries, and other staples. Abundant pictographs, middens, remains of pit-house dwellings, and artifacts attest to the long-term presence of these peoples. Radiocarbon dating of materials found in pit houses at Slocan Junction, just downstream from Bonnington, date back 1700 years. Another pit-house site on Lower Arrow Lake, north of Castlegar, yielded materials that dated back 3200 years.

The Sinixt people harvested kokanee and sockeye with river weirs, J-shaped wicker baskets tied in the water, twisted-bark fish lines with baited wooden hooks, and spears. Like salmon people everywhere, the groups using the Kootenay Lake area dried or smoked part of their catch, producing a highly portable and durable food. Fall harvests of spawners at places like Lasca Creek, the mouth of the Duncan River, and Bonnington Falls were times for reunion, celebration, and ceremony. After feasting, the bones of the fish were carefully wrapped and returned to the water in order to maintain the runs. Such an act may seem quaint and misdirected, until one reflects on its efficacy. Whether it was the custom itself that worked, or the whole suite of fish-harvesting practices in which the custom was embedded, is one of those reductionist scientific questions that may be irrelevant. The fact is, as long as the custom and the practices were followed, the fish kept returning. In contrast, the wheels seem to be coming off our current vaunted fisheries techno-management after only a few decades. More and more, our efforts are directed into desperate rescue measures.

Western ecological knowledge tends toward the quantitative, is packaged in discrete disciplinary parcels, is stored in text, and

The natural resource management agencies within government invest heavily in planning, producing sustainable harvesting plans, land use plans, species recovery plans, and so on. It might be interesting to ask the planners if they think their prescriptions can guarantee 3200 years of resource sustainability.

studiously avoids symbolism and spirituality. In Aboriginal systems, bits of knowledge are connected, qualitative, and are set within the matrix of oral stories. For example, the arrival of kokanee spawning time can be predicted in two ways. Western science does it by monitoring a combination of declining day length and decreasing water temperature. The Sinixt know it is about to occur when sumac leaves turn the fiery red colour of the spawners themselves. There are a number of sound reasons why our respective societies should work toward a greater awareness of each other's knowledge systems, but for me, the strongest logic is simple fascination. I have steeped myself in western scientific knowledge about the kokanee, read the literature and talked to the scientists, but I am still hungry to learn more. Of course I would want to avail myself of another body of knowledge about this fish and its environment.

> *The Sinixt know that spawning time is about to occur when sumac leaves turn the fiery red colour of the spawners themselves.*

The California O'odham elder Dennis Martinez describes this process as "intercultural verification of natural resource states and processes," a comparing of notes, motivated by human fascination with a particular fish or plant or river. Indigenous peoples' knowledge, historically either downgraded or ignored, is now a popular topic and is subject to other forms of abuse. There have been many instances where pharmaceutical interests and academics have violated First Nation intellectual property rights in pursuit of this information. A more subtle form of violation is when non-natives seek out and use specific elements of indigenous peoples' knowledge, but fail to acknowledge the cultural and spiritual matrix of which that knowledge is a part. The typical western approach would be to appropriate all that is known about the medicinal properties of the balsamroot, for example, and then completely ignore the knowledge of balsamroot as a member of the root people.

There is a creation story, told by the Ktunaxa people, that defines the universe of the Kootenays. Before the time of people, a giant lived near Columbia Lake, along with many other spirit animals. A sea monster inhabited the lake, and the monster created no end of problems for the spirit animals. After consultation, the spirit animals and the giant formed a war party to hunt the sea monster down and kill it. The problem was, in those days the waters of the Columbia were joined with the waters of the Kootenay, and the sea monster was able to escape by going down the Kootenay. The war party would give chase, pursuing the monster down the river into present-day Montana, back up through Creston, down the West Arm of Kootenay Lake to Castlegar, and then up the Arrow Lakes. At this point, the party would stop briefly to shoot an arrow at Pierced Rock. If the arrow went through the hole in the rock, they continued chasing the sea monster up to Revelstoke, around the Big Bend, back down through Golden and Invermere, and finally into the lake again. But the monster continued to elude them. The giant and the spirit animals made this great loop many, many times. Finally they stopped, dispirited, as the monster escaped from Columbia Lake yet again. A wise old man sitting on the banks of the lake said to the giant, "Why not use your head and your great strength, and separate the waters of the Columbia from the waters of the Kootenay so next time you and the spirit animals chase the monster, you can trap him in the lake?" The giant did so, and the next time the monster entered the lake, it was trapped. The honour of killing the monster went to the red-headed woodpecker. After it was dispatched, the monster was dragged on shore and the meat was distributed among the animals. The giant took the internal organs, which were various colours, and made them into various races of people. Then he took a handful of grass to wipe off his hands. As he let the bloodstained blades of grass fall to the ground, he decreed that these would become the red people. Immensely pleased with his work, the giant forgot himself and stood up. Banging his head sharply against the sky, he fell down dead and became the Rocky Mountains.

This story, told here in summary form, shows how regional nature is built right into a cultural identity. We, the contempo-

The spirit animals and the giant formed a war party to hunt the sea monster down and kill it.

rary settler culture, still struggle to define who we are and what we mean by the Kootenays. As B.C. writer Harold Rhenisch says, our culture is designed primarily to take over and replace other cultures and seems to lack the critical mass to exist on its own. Perhaps the exercise of building our own mythology will help give us a better sense of this Kootenay region that we share.

Lower Bonnington Dam, 1999. The first hydroelectric dam on the Kootenay River, it was built in 1898. PHOTO BY ART STOCK

Smash and Grab

The universe of the kokanee has been permanently modified by European settlement. Our entry into western Canada was rooted in the discovery, rapid exploitation, and export of natural resources. Even the search for a west-flowing river was ultimately driven by the need to facilitate the shipment of beaver pelts. Settlement of the Kootenay region largely followed the colonial exploitation model, although the first wave, fur trapping, had little impact because of the area's remoteness and mountainous terrain. Where its trappers did find beaver, though, the Hudson's Bay Company was rapacious, intentionally taking all the beaver it could, to discourage competition from American companies.

The second wave, mining, broke more heavily over the area. A gold strike on Wild Horse Creek in the 1860s heralded the beginning of the mining era and caused thousands of people to flock to the East Kootenays. Excavations and tailings piles suddenly appeared everywhere. Streambeds and spawning channels were extensively re-worked as placer miners searched feverishly for gold. Small dams were built to divert water into wooden flumes, to power gravity-fed hydraulic sluicing operations downstream. The integrity and life of streams like Wild Horse and Rock Creek became inconsequential. Streambanks and entire hillsides were sluiced into oblivion.

Shortly after the Wild Horse gold strike, coal was found in the

Fernie basin, and exploitation began there when the railroad arrived in 1898. The 1890s also saw a flurry of lead, zinc, and silver mining activity in the West Kootenays, much of it centred around Kootenay Lake. Nelson, Kaslo, Ainsworth, and Riondel all got their start as mining communities. Here, too, stream channels were blasted, sluiced, cribbed, straightened, and excavated. Small dams were built, forests were logged and burnt, huge quantities of overburden, processed ore, and smelter effluent were dumped into the lake. Miners would intentionally burn off whole mountainsides to better see the rock formations underneath the forest. Early photos of nearly every community in the Kootenays show burned, mine-scarred hillsides in the background. The lush vegetation growth in the West Kootenays covers many of the scars now, but one learns to pick out evidence of old mining activity. Unusual mounds turn out to be piles of overburden, the twisted tree root that trips you turns out to be a rusted length of wire cable, and unexpected pits are early prospector test holes.

Gold mining, from both an ecological and a human perspective, is unstable. Fisherville, the community that sprang from the Wild Horse gold strike, is now abandoned and forgotten. The fabulous gold-mining community of Phoenix, near Grand Forks, once boasted an opera house and a daily newspaper, but lasted only a few decades. Some of these derelict communities originated from mineral strikes that petered out quickly; others were a result of overheated land speculation, outrageous false advertising, and salted claims. Silver, the base metals, and coal, perhaps because of their lesser value, seem to have generated more human stability. Nelson and Riondel, for example, grew up around their silver mines and smelters, and both survived.

Riondel's Bluebell mine came close to destroying the entire food chain of Kootenay Lake. All of Bluebell's overburden was dumped into the adjacent lake, resulting in a concentrated layer of toxic lead in the bottom sediments that remains to this day. Purely by geochemical accident, however, the lead is in a very insoluble form, and it does not get into the food chain.

Consolidated Mining Company, the forerunner of Cominco, began operating the Sullivan lead-zinc mine in Kimberley in 1909 and shipped ore to its smelter in Trail, thus binding the East and West Kootenays in a permanent industrial embrace. The ore was transported along the recently completed Canadian Pacific rail line that ran from Kimberley down the Moyie River valley to Creston, then along the steep shores of Kootenay Lake, down the West Arm, and finally along the Columbia to Trail. Originally all the railway stream crossings were wooden trestles built over unmodified stream channels. As time went on, concrete flumes were poured, eliminating the flood damage that the trestles used to sustain, but also making the portion of the stream above most of these flumes inaccessible to spawning kokanee.

The next wave of exploitation, agriculture, developed into cattle ranching in the East Kootenays, mixed farming on the fertile soils of the Creston Valley, and fruit ranching on the terraces and benches of the West Kootenays. Agriculture's impact on the local landscape was fairly benign, with the notable exception of William Baillie-Grohman's attempt to divert the waters of the Kootenay into the Columbia in the 1880s.

A wealthy Englishman, Baillie-Grohman was either an energetic pioneer visionary or a destructive megalomaniac depending on one's view of history. My father and I never discussed the man, but that would have been an interesting conversation. Baillie-Grohman was convinced that the extensive delta at the south end of Kootenay Lake, known as the Creston Flats, had great potential for settlement, agriculture, and land sale profits. However, the unruly Kootenay River spilled over its banks regularly, leaving the flats underwater, sometimes for weeks at a time. So Baillie-Grohman hatched the scheme of diverting excess floodwater from the Kootenay into the Columbia by digging a canal between the two at a place now known as Canal Flats. In 1888 he actually succeeded in building the diversion canal, using Chinese labourers, but farmers along the upper Columbia River did not view the transfer of flood risk from the Creston Flats to *their* farmlands as a particularly good idea, and they convinced the federal government to intervene on their behalf. Ottawa demanded that Baillie-Grohman install a set of locks on his canal, which would have to stay shut until August of each year. The ever-eager Baillie-Grohman actually did this, but by then his whole canal scheme was bogging down in a morass of siltation and shaky financing. Undaunted, Baillie-Grohman tried again to dry out the Creston Flats, this time from the other direction, by lowering the level of Kootenay Lake. He chose a narrow rapids on the West Arm, just below Nelson. Using barge-mounted steam shovels, he dredged the bottom of the rapids, deepening it, but the quixotic project had little effect on the lake level. A competing land-speculation scheme eventually drove Baillie-Grohman out of business, and he returned to England, defeated.

Logging, the next industrial wave, began as an adjunct to early mining and settlement activity. In the East Kootenays, "tie hacking" — cutting trees for the new transcontinental rail lines — became big business. Virtually all of the old-growth ponderosa pine, larch, and Douglas-fir were removed from the bottom of the Rocky Mountain Trench by the tie hackers. A common early practice was to fell trees, dump them into the larger streams in the area, and wait for the spring freshet to carry them to a downstream sawmill. The scouring effect of these logs meant that many watercourses lost the gravel beds so vital to kokanee and other fish.

The ghost town phenomenon is not restricted to mining; some sawmill-based communities, like Bull River Town, were abandoned when their mills ran out of wood. Timber harvesting in the Kootenays remains today as an important but volatile industry, subject to fluctuating international markets and trade agreements, unrealistically high cut levels, and a host of competing non-timber forest uses.

The next wave of exploitation was that of power generation, a wave we wholeheartedly embraced as a region, a province, and a country. The first hydroelectric dam on the Kootenay River was built at Lower Bonnington Falls in 1898. More followed and by *William Andrew Cecil* 1951 there were 51 dams of significant size registered in the *(W.A.C.) Bennett was* province. Thirty years later the figure topped out at 103. Larger *British Columbia's* dams are typically built for hydroelectric power generation, water *longest-serving premier* storage for downstream hydroelectric dams, flood control, irriga-*(1952–1972) and an* tion, and river transportation.

unapologetic fan of During the W.A.C. Bennett era of the 1960s, the Kootenays *industrial* were assigned the role of the undeveloped, unroaded hinterland, *megaprojects.* to be used for water storage and power generation. Long-time residents of the Kootenay, Arrow, and Pend Oreille valleys were summarily expropriated and their properties were flooded by rising waters behind the new Libby, Keenleyside, and Seven Mile dams.

Along the Kootenay south of Cranbrook, whole communities, like Flagstone and Dorr, disappeared completely under the waters of the Koocanusa reservoir. On the Columbia, Renata was flooded out by the Keenleyside dam, and Edgewood was forced to move to higher ground. Dozens of small farms along the Columbia also disappeared. The actual physical space lost to dams on the Kootenay and Columbia river systems is a small percentage of the landbase, but the ecological loss from the drowning of these productive bottomlands is enormous.

Koocanusa (a contraction of Kootenay-Canada-USA) is faux native, a pathetic attempt at creating a new industrial indigeny. And to call Koocanusa a lake is a grievous misuse of the term.

A dam has a profound impact on the biological life of a river. In the reservoir behind the dam, flow rates slow down, temperatures increase, oxygen levels fall, nutrients settle out and are entombed, water levels no longer rise and fall with the seasons, and as the flushing action of heavy spring flows is attenuated, spawning beds silt in.

Although the major seasonal fluctuations in water levels are reduced, smaller fluctuations occur randomly throughout the year, based on power generation needs. In dammed rivers, high water is never as high, low water is never as low, but day-to-day fluctuations are much greater and are uncoupled from the season. Behind the Seven Mile dam on the Pend Oreille, for example, daily water level fluctuations can be as much as six metres. As a result, the normally diverse foreshore loses all its vegetation, becoming a biological desert. Wind and wave action against this dry, barren strip fouls the adjacent water with silt. This constant, suspended cargo of fine materials prevents light penetration into the normally productive shallow waters, breaking the aquatic food chain at its first link — the photosynthetic algae. Then as the silt settles out, it fills in the gravelly spawning areas, rendering them useless, and there are no spring floods or freshets to strip the gravel clean again. Shore spawning in reservoirs is generally futile, and the exposed and barren mouths of tributaries are hazardous for the creek spawners. Exotic predator fish, like walleye, perch, and pumpkinseed, often thrive in the warm, sluggish water behind dams. It is disturbing to realize that, without consciously intending to do so, we have created structures so totally antithetical to aquatic life.

Healthy, functioning ecosystems depend on a combination of both the predictable and the unpredictable. The predictable sea-

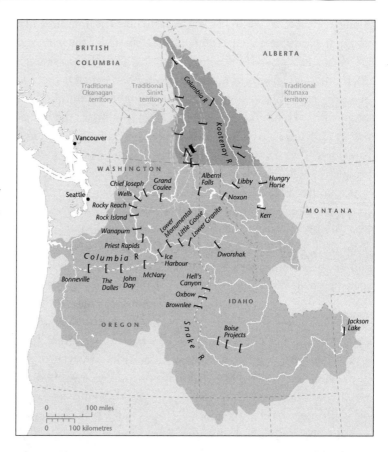

*The Columbia River
basin and dams.*

sonal cycle of rising and falling water levels is punctuated by
occasional unpredictable flood years. Random events overlap to
create these flood years: a high snowfall winter, a cool, wet spring
followed by sudden warming, and then a few days of heavy rain.
When all four of these events coincide, floodwaters start churning
down the mountain creeks, headed for the main rivers and lakes.
1898 was a major flood year. In 1948, downtown Trail was underwater. Spring 1999 was a close call; we had three of the basic conditions for flooding, but the fourth — heavy rain — never came.

Ironically, these unpredictable and destructive floods perform
vital biological functions, scouring accumulated sediments out of
spawning beds, depositing nutrient-rich silt along the foreshore,
and recycling nutrients. After decades of trying to undo the
impacts of floods, fires, storms, and so on, ecologists are beginning to recognize the importance of disturbance in ecosystems.

MAJOR DAMS ON THE COLUMBIA RIVER SYSTEM

This is a partial list, excluding dams on small tributaries and on the upper reaches of large tributaries. Many of these dams were phased in; the date given is for completion of the first phase.

River	Dam	Prov/State	Completed
KOOTENAY			
	Lower Bonnington	BC	1898
	Upper Bonnington	BC	1926
	South Slocan	BC	1928
	Corra Linn	BC	1932
	Brilliant	BC	1944
	Libby	Montana	1972
DUNCAN			
	Duncan	BC	1967
PEND OREILLE			
	Seven Mile	BC	1979
	Albeni Falls	Idaho	1950
	Boundary	Washington	1967
	Box Canyon	Washington	1956
COLUMBIA			
	Grand Coulee	Washington	1933
	Rock Island	Washington	1933
	Bonneville	Washington	1938
	Wanapum	Washington	1944
	McNary	Washington	1957
	The Dalles	Washington	1960
	Chief Joseph	Washington	1961
	Rocky Reach	Washington	1961
	Priest Rapids	Washington	1961
	Wells	Washington	1967
	Keenleyside	BC	1968
	John Day	Washington	1971
	Mica	BC	1973
	Revelstoke	BC	1984
SNAKE RIVER			
	Ice Harbor	Washington	1962
	Lower Monumental	Washington	1969
	Little Goose	Washington	1970
	Lower Granite	Washington	1975

Disturbances in the form of floods are a vital part of the life of a river, a part we have ruthlessly eliminated with dams.

The first major dam on the upper Columbia River system was Grand Coulee, started in 1933 and finished in 1942. A kilometre and a half across, 150 metres thick, and turning 225 kilometres of the Columbia into a stagnant reservoir, it became a symbol for the modern development of the arid west. Its completion marked the beginning of a four-decade frenzy of dam building on both sides of the forty-ninth parallel. Grand Coulee, plus the thirteen other dams that operate on the Columbia's main stem, are all coordinated to maximize power production. Writer Blaine Harden sums it up this way: "The Columbia does not flow, it is operated."

Blaine Harden,
A RIVER LOST:
THE LIFE AND DEATH
OF THE COLUMBIA
(New York: Norton and
Co., 1996).

Our dams are a kind of concrete antithesis of the kokanee, carrying both real and symbolic significance. Dams celebrate our mastery over nature, the power of the engineer and his technologies, the imperial nature of governments and utilities, the ascendancy of consumer needs, and the absolute conviction that natural systems like rivers can be gutted, turned inside out, and then re-engineered to human specifications. Of the many human arrogances that dams have come to symbolize, this last one is perhaps the most catastrophic.

Every dam I know offers free access to the public; the guided tour is part of dam culture. I still remember my first dam tour, to Hoover dam in Nevada, when I was in short pants. Our family travelled there in a tail-finned black 1955 Oldsmobile, and my father, the engineer, provided enthusiastic commentary as we drove the winding road up to the tallest dam in North America, finished in a mad rush in 1936 at the cost of a hundred workers' lives. We stopped at a Scenic Viewpoint just below the dam, and I was dumbstruck by the massive blank wall that loomed above us and by the tomblike quiet.

The inside of Hoover dam was a prototype for all the others I have seen since then, a cross between stationary battleship and industrial church. Small figures move about in obscure tasks among giant and exotic machinery. Everything is rectilinear, curvilinear, and clinical, the exact opposite of the original river channel the dam has replaced. The transformation here is profound: these narrows and falls were once places of abundance, of celebration, of informality, of human exchange; now they are places of biological holocaust, of industrial interdiction, and of group tours from 10 to 3.

No one group is to blame for this, not even the engineers. Dams are us. We excrete them, following the universal forms of concrete morphogenesis, laying down penstocks and caissons the same way whelks at opposite ends of the world lay down calcium and sea water to form the same perfect shells. Dams and hydro-electric generators are cathedrals celebrating the idea of the perfect marriage between technology and nature. They are the deft placement of an additional loop in the grand cycle of water movement from river to ocean to air to river, an addition we thought was perfectly clean and renewable. Everything was in place except ecology, which would have to wait patiently for several decades before we noticed anything had gone wrong.

For those on any dam tour wishing to continue their technological sightseeing, there were usually directions to a nearby fish hatchery. Salmon hatcheries developed as adjuncts to dams. The complementary dam and hatchery technologies would allow us, or so we convinced ourselves, to sacrifice the river but keep the salmon. With salmon spawning runs going extinct in some rivers and in trouble everywhere, hatchery technology as a solution to declining wild salmon stocks is now largely discredited.

The heyday of dam construction began in the 1930s. In a single decade, from 1960 to 1970, six major dams were completed on the main stem of the Columbia, and two more on the Snake. By the late 1970s we woke up to decide that even though we could start another one tomorrow if we wanted to, maybe we had enough dams for the time being. The Revelstoke dam, completed in 1984, was the last dam built on the Columbia watershed. Now, a hundred years into the hydro dam era, some people are openly discussing taking some of them down. In 2002, people in southeastern Washington and adjacent Idaho are locked into an agonizing debate about removing four dams on the lower Snake River. Salmon vs. jobs is the issue, and given the present pathetic state of the Snake salmon runs and the healthy shipping, irrigated farming, and hydro power that the dams facilitate, the outcome is an open-and-shut case.

In 1956 a dam was built on the Theodosia River on B.C.'s south coast, diverting three-quarters of the river's flow into an

See Jim Lichatowich, SALMON WITHOUT RIVERS *(Covelo, CA: Island Press, 1999).*

impoundment for a hydro plant, and devastating the river's salmon runs. The structure is due to be removed soon, the first removal of a major dam in British Columbia. The Theodosia could become a living laboratory for the resurrection of a river.

My father was deeply offended by the hippie movement of the 1960s, particularly by its rejection of technological progress and established values, not to mention the hair. I in turn, as part of that movement, was deeply offended by technology and established values, not to mention Vietnam. When our mutual affronts had weathered down to the point that my father and I could talk again, the condition of rivers, oceans, lakes, and fishing was generally a safe area for conversation. On our rare meetings I would probe on those issues to gauge the reactions of this hard-edged man. For a time he lived in northern California, near a rusting Louisiana-Pacific pulp mill, which regularly polluted the saltwater bay it sat in with a toxic, foul-smelling effluent. Testing him, I mentioned how destructive LP's dumping practice must be to the fish habitat. He responded by saying, "You're damn right, it's a terrible thing, and whenever anyone makes any noise about it, LP just threatens to close down the mill and put people out of work."

I absorbed that statement in stunned silence. From this oracle of conservative, establishment, and technocratic values came a shocking bit of ecopolitical analysis. I look back on that comment as a belated endorsement and a kind of cross-generational mandate. If the condition of rivers, lakes, oceans, and salmonids made my earth-moving, engineer father say that, then they were indeed in bad shape and I had better act on that endorsement. In the confused tangle of our lives together, my father had found a free end and offered it to me.

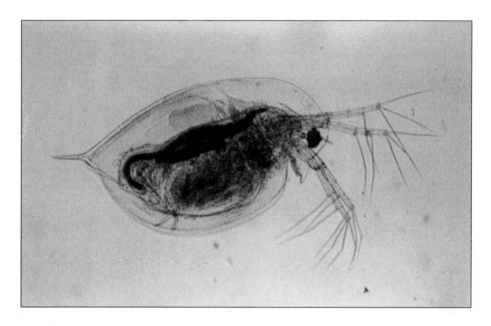

Daphnia pulex, the microscopic creature at the base of an 8,000-year-old food chain that sustains the kokanee. PHOTO BY BERT LORO

The Engine of Life

Kootenay Lake has a simple and elegant food chain. Microscopic algae feed on sunlight and nutrients dissolved in the water. Daphnia, a pudgy little invertebrate, feed on the algae. Kokanee feed on the Daphnia. Gerrard rainbows and bull trout feed on the kokanee. Ospreys and bears feed on rainbows and kokanee. With the exception of a few minor microbial side links, that is basically the chain. Individual links may have been forged earlier, but the algae / Daphnia / kokanee / Gerrard / osprey / bear chain is relatively new, perhaps only 8000 years old.

The beginning of the food chain is sunlight, water, oxygen, and moderate temperatures, all of which are abundant in Kootenay Lake. The real chokepoint in the lake's food chain is the next link — the nutrient supply. It is always difficult to translate ecology into biochemistry, from the reality of an osprey grabbing a spawned-out kokanee to the abstraction of molecules, of parts-per-billion, of N-P-K, of nitrate this and oxide that. But N-P-K (nitrogen, phosphorous, potassium, and their host of derived compounds) is what the kokanee hoards and the osprey seeks. These nutrients are what food chains are all about. Perhaps one day the biochemists will be able to create a virtual reality for us so we can watch the invisible ebb and flow of nutrient molecules between species. For now, most of us take N-P-K on faith, on the overwhelming evidence of cause and effect and by the way it perks up our roses.

Kootenay Lake is considered oligotrophic (oligo=few, troph=level), the unlovely term for an ecosystem with few nutrients. Rivers and streams that feed the lake come from steep, rocky lands and have little opportunity to absorb nutrients from either dissolving bedrock or rotting vegetation. Biologists describe the mountains around Kootenay Lake as having "recalcitrant lithology," which means they are hard granites, reluctant to dissolve and give up their cargo of nutrients. At the other end of the scale, the Qu'Appelle Lakes of Saskatchewan are biological hotrods by comparison; shallow, receiving runoff from level, fertile soils, they are warm, "eutrophic," and support massive algae blooms in midsummer.

The notable exception to the nutrient-poor inflows to Kootenay Lake is the Kootenay River. Carving through the relatively rich glacial sediments and gentler terrain of the Rocky Mountain Trench, the Kootenay flows have the opportunity to enrich themselves with nutrients. Those nutrients have historically been vital to the lake's food chain.

Kootenay Lake was frozen deeper into natural oligotrophy by Lower Bonnington, when the falls cut off the transfer of marine nutrients to fresh water by way of the sockeye. Lakes such as Shuswap, which still have unrestricted salmon passage to and from the Pacific, tend to have better nutrient status and greater biodiversity.

The modern irony of an oligotrophic lake in a densely settled area like the West Kootenay is the ready availability of phosphorous and nitrogen tied up in human waste. Were it not for the modern human scourges of concentration, disease, and pollutants, we too could form a productive part of the kokanee food chain.

When river and stream waters arrive in Kootenay Lake, their small cargo of nutrients is diluted in a massive, deep waterbody. Nutrients that happen to sink below thirty metres are generally lost from the system, permanently entombed in bottom sediments. The average depth of this lake is 100 metres, so there is ample opportunity for nutrients to drop out of circulation. As a result, life in Kootenay Lake is basically a quest for scarce nutrients. The scarcest, most powerful of all of these is phosphorous. A typical cell will have 102 carbon molecules and 16 nitrogen molecules for every molecule of phosphorous. Biological systems are normally awash with carbon, and most have sufficient nitrogen; phosphorous is the element they wait anxiously for. Upon entry into a biological cycle, phosphorous is immediately used in the creation of complex molecules. Key among the phosphorous products is adenosine triphosphate, ATP, the molecule that carries nerve impulses in living organisms. So universal is ATP in living systems that when biologists attempt to measure the amount of microbial activity in soil, they find it far easier to simply extract ATP and then use a standard conversion formula to determine biomass.

It is hard to believe that an organism barely visible to the naked eye is the primary food of the kokanee.

When a phosphorous molecule is ripped from the durable granites of Fry Creek or Gray Creek and tumbled down the mountain into the lake, it is immediately vacuumed up by one of two aquatic diatoms with names like fairy-tale princesses: Fragilaria and Asterionella. These diatoms, a form of algae encased in exquisitely delicate silica capsules, are the primary producers at the very bottom of the food chain, the ones that combine sunlight and nutrients to produce the living tissue that all other animals depend on. These humble algae are then preyed upon by Daphnia and other invertebrates that make up the class of organisms we know as lake plankton. Looking for all the world like a pudgy character from a morning TV show for children, Daphnia doodles about the surface waters, searching for algae, which it waves into its gut with a series of mouthparts that operate like an eggbeater. It is hard to believe that an organism barely visible to the naked eye is the primary food of the kokanee, but consider the massive sperm whale, which feeds entirely on the marine equivalents of the Daphnia. The only difference is that kokanee search for and take one Daphnia at a time, whereas the whales can sieve out huge quantities of plankton through their baleen plates.

I spend a lot of time looking at the waters of Kootenay Lake and the West Arm, and I never see algae mats or blooms of Daphnia. Both organisms are there, but they are highly dispersed, in vanishingly small quantities.

Some obscure motive prompted me to start a home aquarium in the midst of my kokanee investigations, and I found unexpected resonances between the two. My starting context for this hobby was the round goldfish bowl I maintained as a kid, which had a layer of second-rank marbles on the bottom (the good ones I kept in a pouch on my belt) and got its water changed twice a year, whether it needed it or not. This time around I was confronted by full-blown aquarium science, with dauntingly sophisticated biological and mechanical filtration, bacterial additives, aeration, high-powered lighting, nutrient test kits, and rigorous maintenance regimes. To do it right, following the extensive and contradictory directions in aquarium manuals, took me several hours per week. All this for thirty gallons of water in the corner of our living room. I had a sliver of realization about what it meant to be a limnologist or fisheries biologist on Kootenay Lake.

Adding phosphorus for Kokanee fishery, 1996. A pair of huge fertilizer tanks are mounted on a barge. The wake of the pusher tug helps disperse the phosphorus in the lake water. PHOTO BY ART STOCK

A Chronicle of
Interference

In the spring of 1949, Peter Larkin of the B.C. government's Game Commission made a trip to Waterton Lake, Alberta. He felt that the fishery at Kootenay Lake was not reaching its full potential, and he had an idea how to enhance it. Using a fine-meshed net, he trawled the bottom of Waterton Lake and captured a small population of a tiny crustacean called Mysis and its even more diminutive cousin, Pontoporeia. These two organisms were found in Waterton and other lakes east of the Rockies, but not in B.C. lakes. Larkin's idea was that Mysis (also known as the "opossum shrimp," for its nocturnal habits) and Pontoporeia would be an ideal food source for the Gerrard rainbows of Kootenay Lake. The Gerrards feed on plankton when they are fry, then switch to a diet of kokanee once they are mature. Larkin felt that the two crustaceans might become an intermediate food source that would help the growing rainbows as they moved from juvenile to adult food. Accordingly, he released Mysis and Pontoporeia into Kootenay Lake in 1949 and again in 1950.

As the newcomers slowly worked their way into the lake's ecology, biologists duly included them in their periodic monitoring regime. Kootenay Lake is remarkable in many ways, but one of the unique aspects of this rather remote mountain lake is its lengthy legacy of monitoring. Beginning as early as the 1930s, scientists from as far away as Ontario have made the trek to the lake

The Secchi disk is a delightfully simple instrument for measuring water clarity. A black-and-white painted disk attached to a calibrated rope, it is lowered into the water until it can no longer be seen, at which point the depth is recorded.

with their sample bottles, Secchi disks, and trawling nets, making the time-consuming and often tedious measurements that form the basis of limnology, the scientific study of inland waters. The natural splendour of the lake may in some way be responsible for this great scientific legacy, and we should take comfort in the knowledge that some scientists are affected by beauty.

For the first several years, Larkin's species introductions were written off as a failure since the monitoring found no Pontoporeia at all, and Mysis in only small quantities. This was not unexpected. In the lengthy history of aquatic introductions around North America, certain species caught on and others didn't, and it was hard to predict outcomes in advance.

Far off in the East Kootenay community of Kimberley, another interference was taking place. In 1953, Cominco's massive Sullivan lead-zinc mine began producing phosphate fertilizer as a byproduct. In the industrial style of the day, the fertilizer plant was a messy operation, producing large quantities of phosphorous-laced wastewater, which was dumped unceremoniously into the adjacent Saint Mary's River. Tumbling down the rapids of the Saint Mary's and into the Kootenay River system, this concentrated pulse of phosphorous acted like an ecological steroid. Quickly snapped up by ravening algae and spiralled upward into Kootenay Lake's food chain, Cominco's phosphorous boosted kokanee numbers as well as their size at maturity. By 1962, fertilizer production was in full swing. Phosphorous fertilizer tonnage, as well as phosphorous pollution, increased steadily to a peak in 1967. Around Kootenay Lake, people noticed a decrease in the renowned clarity of the lake's water, and during hot summers, floating algae mats appeared, which no one could remember seeing before.

Meanwhile, the Mysis had been biding its time in the lake, slowly adapting to the conditions of its new home. In the early 1960s it began to show up in the monthly monitoring reports, and scientists belatedly realized that the Mysis transplant had indeed been successful.

At about this same time, the diminutive kokanee, not considered a sport fish because of its small size, and thought of mainly as food for the Gerrard rainbows, began a radical transformation. The herring-sized kokanee were now achieving lengths up to 45 centimetres and weights of 3.5 kilograms, nearly as large as their saltwater cousins. The kokanee's fine red flesh and sportiness made them a welcome addition to the creels of both local and visiting anglers, who now could fish for the big Gerrards as well as chase the bulked-up kokanee.

Word about good fishing in Kootenay Lake spread through the angler's grapevine, and fishing pressure began to concentrate around Balfour, where the lake flows into the West Arm. Fishers from Washington and Idaho began making regular annual pilgrimages to Balfour, which now boasted ten different fishing resorts. Osprey fought over the opportunity to nest on the pilings of the strategically located Balfour ferry dock, even though it meant getting jostled, stared at, and photographed every hour on the half hour. Local legend has it that neophyte tourist fishers would occasionally tie their boats to one of the pilings, shortly thereafter to receive a copious and vile-smelling christening from that piling's resident osprey.

Peter Larkin was belatedly applauded for his pioneering Mysis work. The media picked up the story, and soon Mysis was the instant solution for overfished and unproductive lakes. Based on the Kootenay Lake example, Mysis introductions were made in Okanagan Lake, the Arrow Lakes, and several other lakes in B.C., the United States, and even Scandinavia.

By the early seventies, however, the Mysis data began to set off alarm bells in the scientific community. The shrimp were now multiplying rapidly and feeding on Daphnia, the primary food of the kokanee, yet very few Mysis were showing up in the guts of either rainbows or kokanee. The normal algae to Daphnia to kokanee to rainbow food chain was being disrupted by what the biologists dubbed "the Mysis shunt," which was algae to Daphnia to Mysis, period. In other words, the Mysis were happily consuming, but rarely being consumed. Exploring further, the scientists stumbled onto a fundamental problem: the daily migrations of the light-shy Mysis were completely out of phase with the daily movements of both kokanee and rainbows. The cagey, opossum-like shrimp would rise at nightfall to feed and then migrate back down to great depths to avoid predation during the day. The fish, in their turn, carried out the opposite diurnal migration, feeding in the surface layers in the mornings and moving to intermediate depths later in the day and at night. Because of the great depth of Kootenay Lake, the Mysis were able to avoid being eaten by either kokanee or rainbow.

Gut samples of fish from various locations confirmed this: Mysis were successfully avoiding predation everywhere in the lake, except at a single location. The fish of the Balfour–Queens Bay area, at the lake's outlet, were actively consuming Mysis. The reason soon became obvious. With an average depth of 100 metres, the main lake provided abundant opportunity for the Mysis to sink out of reach of fish predators, but those shrimp that drifted by the lake's outlet were swept into the current and then trapped in the shallow confines of the ten- to thirty-metre-deep West Arm outlet, where nightly deep migrations were impossible. Any Mysis that were carried into the West Arm became easy pickings for the local kokanee population. The "Balfour sill," as it became known, was like the shallow overflow drain of the deep Kootenay Lake bathtub, making the narrow stretch of river the most popular fishing spot — for both people and osprey — in the entire lake system.

As the biologists examined their reams of lake and fish data, a new and disturbing picture emerged. They realized the Mysis was actually not responsible for the overall enhancement of the fishery, except in the unique situation at the Balfour sill. Cominco's phosphorous pollution was in fact the main engine behind the increase, and the Mysis introduction was actually a tragic mistake.

Not long after Mysis and Cominco, a further interference was added to this already complex and volatile mix. Following the signing of the 1964 Columbia River Treaty, British Columbia built a dam on the Duncan River, which flows into the north end of Kootenay Lake. The Duncan was a "drone" dam, with no hydroelectric-generating capacity; its purpose was strictly downstream flood control and water storage. The dam on the Duncan disrupted North Arm kokanee spawning habitat, but more critically, it cut off the vital flow of nutrients into the lake, entombing them in reservoir sediments behind the new dam. The Duncan dam also caused the extinction of the Gerrard's twin, the large Duncan rainbow trout, plus millions of kokanee. Then in 1972, Libby dam was installed across the Kootenay River near the bot-

The Columbia River Treaty is a complex and revealing U.S.–Canadian agreement that involves flood control, fisheries, hydroelectric power, and political power.

tom of its southward loop into Montana. This dam, also built under the terms of the Columbia River Treaty, administered the *coup de grâce* for the artificially inflated kokanee fishery. The long stretch of dead water (Koocanusa reservoir) created behind the Libby dam caused virtually all the nutrients to settle out, not only those from the Cominco plant, but the naturally occurring ones as well.

In a final and ironic twist to the story, settling ponds were finally installed at the Cominco fertilizer plant in 1969, removing most of the phosphorous from the wastewater, and in 1987 the fertilizer plant was shut down altogether.

Cut off from its phosphorous supply and disrupted by the Mysis, the lake's food chain started into freefall. Kokanee escapement (the number of adult spawners returning to a given location) in the North Arm of the lake had ramped up to over a million in the peak year of 1977; by 1991 it was down to a quarter of a million. The South Arm stocks, always the most vulnerable of the three, became virtually extinct. The kokanee-dependent Gerrard rainbows, the trophy fish of Kootenay Lake, suffered much the same fate. Fishing success rates dropped dramatically. The same charter, tackle, moorage, food, and accommodation businesses that had done so well during the phosphorous pollution years were now either out of business or complaining loudly. "What happened to the vaunted Mysis solution? Why isn't it working?" they asked.

The scientists who had worked on the lake over the years were called in and began poring over data on nutrient loading, temperature gradients, zooplankton, Mysis, and fish escapement, looking for a solution. One unique proposal that came out of this process, and which was actually seriously considered, was to install a string of swimming pool lights along the bottom of the lake. The light would drive the Mysis back up toward the surface, where they could be eaten by fish. Another blue-sky proposal was to install a giant circular air bubbler on the bottom, creating an upward current that would sweep helpless Mysis into the waiting jaws of kokanee and juvenile Gerrards. However, one of the mathematically inclined scientists pulled out a calculator and showed that a bubbler of a scale large enough to bring shrimp to the surface would not only be prohibitively expensive, but might also create a huge downward current powerful enough to suck in canoes and water-skiers.

The breakthrough came when Dr. Carl Walters, an ecological modelling specialist at the University of British Columbia (UBC), was asked to develop a model of the lake to test various restoration options. Mathematical modelling of ecosystems is a relatively young child of the computer age. To build a model, the various organisms and forces acting in an ecosystem, and their interactions with each other, are documented. Quantitative levels and rates and thresholds are assigned to each element, and formulae are derived for the interactions. Then the model, which lives as a computer program and in huge piles of printouts, is "grown," or allowed to run for a time, while the reactions of key elements are watched. Walters and a team of graduate students built the preliminary model.

One of the key options the modellers wanted to test was the concept of fertilizing the lake. The idea was not new; in fact it had been proposed decades earlier by Peter Larkin, the same biologist whose introductions contributed to the fishery collapse. The irony of reviving Larkin's fertilization proposal was not lost on the researchers, but thanks to the long-term monitoring they had solid evidence showing that current lake phosphorous levels were not only lower than what they had been before the Libby and Duncan dams went into operation, but were actually lower than they had been prior to the start of Cominco's fertilizer plant operations. In other words, the undisturbed, pre-industrial Kootenay river and lake system had a certain natural annual input of phosphorous derived from bedrock, rotting vegetation, and other sources, but because of the dams, the current level was about one-third of that historical level and was dropping steadily. The kokanee food chain was about to shatter.

Dr. Walter's modelling team included Ken Ashley, a keen young limnologist stationed at the Ministry of Environment's research section at UBC. Walters, Ashley, and a heterogeneous collection of Kootenay Lake specialists gathered at UBC in the spring of 1991 to test the model. Walters used a concept called "fast modelling," where the scientists are asked for crude estimates of amounts, rates, and thresholds for each component of the model.

That data is entered, the model is run, and after the laughter at the first results subsides, the scientists try to determine what input numbers or what part of the model is wrong. Amendments are made for a second iteration, the model is run, and the process continues.

Once the model seemed to be running smoothly, the fertilization option was tested, but the results were not encouraging. When virtual phosphorous was added to the virtual lake, the crafty Mysis came out the clear winner, not the kokanee, and not the rainbows that depended on them. The scientists rechecked their data and ran the model again, with the same result. The infamous Mysis shunt was at work in the model; algae ate the added phosphorous, Daphnia ate the increased algae, Mysis ate the increased Daphnia, but then nothing ate the increased Mysis. Other management options seemed even less promising. Restocking with hatchery kokanee would just mean putting more fish into an already famished lake. And although local residents knew the lake was in trouble, they wouldn't take kindly to a total closure of the fishery.

The scientists were at a crossroads: should they attempt an expensive, unproven, and potentially risky fertilization project, or should they stand by and watch an entire food chain collapse? Based on some earlier fertilization research, Ken Ashley had a gut feeling it might work in spite of the modelling results, and he urged the group to try it. Ashley remembers the crucial moment well. "We had talked about every possible aspect of the fertilization, and we were just sitting there, silent and grim-faced, when Harvey Andrusak, the regional manager of the Fish and Wildlife Branch, turned to me and said, 'Well, can you fix this goddamn lake or not?' I swallowed hard, and said yes."

Ashley returned to his laboratory and spent days agonizing over what a practical fertilization project might cost. When he was finished, he phoned Andrusak. "Harvey, I've got a number for you," Ashley said, "but you better sit down first before you hear it." He breathed a number close to half a million dollars.

There was a long pause and then Andrusak replied, "Ashley, it's your job to fix the lake, and it's my job to find you the money. So quit wasting my time and order the fertilizer."

With support from the fledgling Columbia Basin Fish and

The Columbia Basin Fish and Wildlife Compensation Program is a partnership between BC Hydro and the Ministry of Environment, Lands and Parks (now Water, Land and Air Protection) to conserve and enhance fish and wildlife populations affected by BC Hydro dams in the Columbia Basin.

Wildlife Compensation Program, the Fish and Wildlife Branch approved a five-year pilot fertilization experiment. It was to be the largest lake-fertilization project ever undertaken anywhere. A pair of huge fertilizer tanks were mounted on a barge with a pusher tug behind it, and beginning in April 1992 this bizarre craft, with a mixture of dissolved phosphorous and nitrogen in its tanks, made a weekly ten-kilometre run down the middle of the North Arm of Kootenay Lake, dribbling the mixture overboard at a predetermined rate. The prop wash of the tug served to distribute the fertilizer, which infused into the lake at an initial rate of eight metric tonnes per week. As the water warmed and biological activity increased through the summer, the fertilizer application rate rose to over eighty tonnes, then ramped back down toward the last delivery in late August. The ratio of phosphorous to nitrogen varied throughout the season as well. Phosphorous and nitrogen are like the yin and yang of microbial nutrition. Green algae need both nutrients, but there is another, less-desirable form of algae, the blue-green algae, that develops in late summer and is able to capture its own nitrogen from the air. By reducing the amount of phosphorous in late summer, the blue-greens can be held in check.

The scientific community held its collective breath and waited for the results. Contrary to the outcome predicted by the model, the kokanee did respond positively to fertilization. By 1994, fish escapement from the North Arm had rebounded to mid-1980s levels. Overall, the lake went from 150 kokanee per hectare in 1991 to 800 per hectare in 1999. The Gerrard rainbows and bull trout benefited as well; a local fishermen's "Twenty-Pound Club" jumped from two to twenty-six members.

Modeller Carl Walters, who went on to work with many other aquatic systems around the world, supports the Kootenay Lake modelling process, even though its predictions were incorrect. "It was a good exercise," he said, "and it got all of the scientists on Kootenay Lake to really focus on the key issues and approach the actual fertilizer trial on a much more analytical basis."

In comparing the modelling results with the actual fertilization results, the scientists realized there was an upper limit to the size of the Mysis population, a kind of ceiling, which they suspected was due to cannibalism. A second, more important, realization was that the number of eggs that each spawning kokanee produced jumped dramatically in the first few years after fertilization, from an average of 250 eggs per spawner up to nearly 400. However, as this population bulge worked its way through the food chain, egg numbers soon dropped back to pre-fertilization levels.

At the end of the five-year experiment, Ashley and fellow Kootenay fisheries biologists Jay Hammond and Bob Lindsay decided to push the envelope; they intentionally reduced the amount of fertilizer going into the lake and put the fish population at risk. In 1997 they cut the amount of phosphorous by 40 percent, and in 1998 and 1999 by 50 percent. The effect was immediate, and kokanee stocks began a downward spiral. In 2001, fertilization was restored to the original levels, and fish stocks began to rebuild again.

Ashley is quick to defend the fertilizer reduction experiment. "Some of the nay-sayers, including Carl Walters, suggested we just 'got lucky' in 1992 to 1996, and we had no conclusive proof of the validity of lake fertilization," he says. "So the lessons we learned from the 1997 to 2000 period were just as important as the lessons from 1992 to '96. For a scientist, there is nothing more compelling than undoing what you've already done and then re-doing it, to prove that the changes you saw actually happened because of your treatment and not because of some random event."

Another compulsion of the wildlife biologist, and indeed of many of us, is to make a brief, surgical intervention into damaged nature so that it may go on to fix itself. The fertilization project was not destined to be one of those interventions. As long as Mysis are in Kootenay Lake, and the Duncan and Libby dams rob the lake of its natural nutrient inputs, some form of fertilization will be required to sustain the food chain and the fishery.

I first arrived in Nelson just as the Kootenay Lake fertilization program was being proposed, and I was deeply offended by it. Knowing nothing of the local situation, but having had my fill of decades of industrial solutions to ecological problems (problems largely caused by industrial development to begin with), I went storming into the Ministry of Environment office, demanding to talk to a fisheries person. Jay Hammond, the regional fisheries biologist, received me and patiently walked me through the basics of the phosphorous history of Kootenay Lake. An hour later I had the picture and remember making the comment, "So there's really only three options here. Either you let the fishery die, you blow up Libby dam, or you fertilize."

The scientists have also turned their attention to fertilizing the Arrow Lakes reservoir, where the kokanee and their local nemesis, the rare yellow-fin rainbow, are also in steep decline. Upper Arrow Lake, between Revelstoke and Nakusp, is in the worst shape, with only about 60 kokanee per hectare. Ashley acknowledges that the Arrow will be a much tougher challenge than Kootenay Lake, as the whole Columbia system is much more heavily impacted by dams. As Ashley describes it, with two dams upstream and one downstream, the Arrow Lakes reservoir is slowly, inexorably, running out of gas. However, early indications are that the Arrow Lakes will respond positively to fertilization, much the way Kootenay Lake did.

Upper Arrow Lake is in the worst shape, with only about 60 kokanee per hectare.

The Kootenay Lake phosphorous story, as well as the Libby dam experience, are ecological moral tales, modern fables. Like that old tale of the Tar Baby, they show that once we touch a system, it seems we have to keep on touching it. When we have damaged an ecosystem (a river, for instance) with technology (a dam), we may have to use more technology (fertilization) to repair it. This runs counter to a strong current in contemporary thinking, which is that the best way to manage or repair an ecosystem is to leave it alone. The Kootenay Lake experience suggests a different, more interventionist paradigm.

The Mysis tale is a parallel one, teaching us a history lesson. It is easy to condemn Peter Larkin for an unwise and destructive biological introduction, to write him off as an unthinking ecological cowboy. It is more difficult, but more instructive, to recognize that he was a well-respected scientist at the time, that he was following a lengthy tradition of purposeful alien biological introductions into Kootenay Lake, and that his example was eagerly copied by his peers across North America. As Tom Northcote, another early Game Commission biologist, admitted, they were looking for a "quick fix," and the Mysis seemed to be it. What we don't learn from we are condemned to repeat. What sophisticated and widely accepted ecosystem management practice are we employing now that will be ridiculed and disparaged fifty years hence?

Carl Walters feels that Larkin's Mysis experiment actually represented the best thinking of the time and that the idea of filling a perceived gap in the food chain was innovative and imaginative. The problem, Walters says, was that scientists were focussed on "first-order" impacts on ecosystems and had no understanding of second-order, indirect effects. Walters does fault Larkin for not asking the obvious question about Mysis while it was still confined to Waterton, its home lake: If this shrimp is such perfect fish food, why is it so rarely eaten?

Another Mysis tale originates from Flathead Lake in western Montana, a similar cold, oligotrophic, Mysis-free mountain lake. Kokanee were not native to the lake, but were introduced in 1916 and caught on reasonably well as a game fish. Following on the heels of Peter Larkin's Kootenay Lake project, Mysis were introduced into Flathead Lake in the late 1960s to bolster kokanee production. The Mysis introduction backfired in the Flathead the same way it did in Kootenay Lake, but the backfire sent a destructive ripple on up the food chain. McDonald Creek, the major kokanee spawning area for Flathead Lake, hosted one of the largest concentrations of bald eagles in North America, a concentration that coincided with the kokanee spawning run. The Mysis-induced kokanee crash caused a corresponding crash in bald eagle populations along McDonald Creek.

It could be argued that the bald eagle numbers were artificially inflated by the introduction of the kokanee, and the Mysis introduction somehow balanced this out. But then one might take into account previous bald eagle food sources that we have already eliminated, such as bison carcasses or all the salmon spawners that once swam the entire Columbia drainage basin prior to the dams.

Folktales and children's stories help ease young people into the complex and ambiguous world of adult life. Perhaps these ecological moral tales of fish, shrimp, and birds can help ease us adults into the complex and ambiguous world of living with nature, rather than in spite of it. They help us understand that ecosystems are complex, our actions upon them are far-reaching, human arrogance comes at a price, and we are not godlike in our wisdom.

Biological introductions, like that of the Mysis, are having a profound impact on the earth's ecology. The rate of purposeful and accidental introductions is rapidly turning us, in the words of David Quammen, into a planet of weeds. The net effect is a kind of homogenization, a franchising of the world's ecology, with the most aggressive, adaptable species, the starlings and the cheat-grasses and their equivalents, dominant everywhere. Look at the record of purposeful fish introductions into the Kootenay Lake system: yellow perch (1890); Atlantic salmon (1911); coastal cut-throat trout (1911); brook trout (1915); largemouth bass (1916); pumpkinseed (unknown); lake whitefish (1930); rainbow trout (1940s). The complement to these gratuitous introductions is a long tradition of gratuitous removal, of taking eggs and fry of Kootenay Lake kokanee and Gerrard rainbow and stocking them elsewhere.

David Quammen, "A Planet of Weeds," in HARPERS MAGAZINE, *October 1998, pp. 57-69.*

Even the celebrated angler and writer Roderick Haig-Brown got in on the act. "Since there is in Kootenay Lake . . . an abun-dance of forage fish not at present utilized, the desirability of planting some large predator, such as one or the other of the bass or the pike or the muskellunge, is well worth considering." Fortu-nately, Haig-Brown's idea was not acted on.

Roderick Haig-Brown, THE WESTERN ANGLER *(New York: William Morrow & Co., 1947).*

The ignorance and hubris underlying such introductions are perhaps shocking now, but they weren't when the introductions were proposed. Some would say that the only way the human species can learn is through mistakes, but the natural world seems to always pay the price of those learning experiences, and there is a limit to the number of mistakes it can absorb.

Ecology has very few hard and fast laws, but there is one eco-logical rule that approaches physics in its rigorous simplicity: Successful alien species introductions, whether they are purpose-ful or accidental, are irreversible. The only alternative is the expensive and painfully slow process of seeking out biological control agents that are specific to the alien introduction, and even then elimination is never achieved, only suppression. There are no bio-control agents on the horizon for the crafty Mysis, but there have been experimental attempts at harvesting them. Okanagan Lake Mysis are currently being frozen and marketed as tropical fish food, but it will take a lot of aquaria to even make a dent in the population.

The Kootenay Lake Mysis introduction is an ecological puzzle. Both the source lake of the shrimp and the destination lake are deep, cold, and oligotrophic, and they are only a few hundred kilometres apart. Why wasn't Mysis found naturally in Kootenay Lake, and why is it not destructive to fish populations in its native Waterton Lake?

The answer involves glaciers, mountains, and time. The Mysis originated as a marine shrimp, roaming the frigid waters of Hudson Bay. As the last Ice Age began, the continent-spanning Laurentian Glacier got its start in the bay, and as it expanded south and west across the prairies, it actually pushed a saltwater proglacial lake in front of it. That moving saltwater lake contained a host of species, most of which died off, but a few did survive the transition from Arctic salt water to mid-continent fresh water. Among the survivors were the lake trout and the Mysis. One can virtually map the southern extent of the Laurentian Glacier by examining the natural distribution of these two species. The Mysis is native to deep lakes in Canada east of the Rockies, the Great Lakes, and a few lakes in upstate New York. As massive as the glacier was, though, it was unable to cross the Rocky Mountain barrier. Kootenay Lake was of course also covered by ice, but from a different glacier system, the Cordilleran, which did not originate in salt water. So Waterton Lake, which still sends its outflow back to Hudson Bay, never hosted spawning salmon, and its resident fish have had 10,000 years to figure out how to coexist with the Mysis.

I look forward to the day when we reach full ecological literacy, when high-school students devote as much time to the Kootenay Lake Mysis introduction as they do to the Treaty of Versailles, and food chains are discussed at the dinner table.

An osprey near Lasca Creek, a major kokanee spawning run, where the water is transparent, making the redfish easy to spot. PHOTO BY ART STOCK

Home Water

M y oldest son and I settled into our boat, which was the marine equivalent of a 1965 Chevrolet pickup, and eased it down the West Arm toward Grohman Creek. We chose our route carefully, since the bottle-green water of this stretch hides many hazards fatal to expensive propellers. Passing close to a sheer rock face, we looked at fading Aboriginal pictographs, set high above water level. Ivan was visiting and agreed to accompany me on my informal fall survey of kokanee spawning in the creeks of the lower West Arm. I didn't want to risk the propeller by going farther downstream, so we beached the boat on some coarse gravel above the mouth of Grohman Creek and then trudged down a curious low, flat ridge that ran parallel to the shore. Scrubby aspen and lodgepole grew out of the ridge's stony slopes, but there was something unnatural about this landform. We were nearly to the end of the half-kilometre-long ridge when it suddenly dawned on me. This was the old spoil pile from William Baillie-Grohman's Homeric dredging project, in which he attempted to lower the entire Kootenay River system. We marvelled at the man's obsessiveness.

There is something about rocks above water that challenges you to see if you can balance on them without falling in. Grohman Creek was full of rounded, half-submerged boulders, strewn in patterns just a short leap apart. Ivan and I picked our way along, each following a different path, trusting our ankles. It was a guy thing. I scanned the pools ahead of me as I balanced and skipped, balanced and skipped. There were no kokanee. In fact, I didn't see any gravel beds that were suitable for spawning. Somewhere I had read that salmonids prefer gravel with an average diameter about 10 percent of their body length, so the kokanee would be happy with golf-ball-sized gravels, and everything in Grohman Creek was far larger than that. We crowhopped upstream for several hundred metres before finally stopping. There were no fish. At best, this creek would be a minor contributor to the overall spawning pool, but still, it seemed significant that it did not host a single spawner.

Was the absence of fine gravels the result of human activity? Was it because of Baillie-Grohman's insane scheme of a century before? Did a blowout flood sweep all the gravels away? Is the natural gradient of Grohman Creek simply too steep to hold small gravel? Will kokanee spawn this far away from the main lake? These all seemed like good and useful questions to explore.

However complex the kokanee's origins might be, its reproductive cycle is fairly straightforward. In the third or fourth fall of their existence, kokanee leave the main lake and return unerringly to their natal stream to mate once and die. The fertilized eggs gestate over winter in their matrix of specially selected gravel. Then on a rainy, moonless spring night, the recently hatched fry make the perilous dash down to the main lake. Three or four years later, the few percent left of that original fry cohort returns to the same stream to repeat the process.

After the day's venture to Grohman, Ivan had to return to his bush work on Vancouver Island, leaving me to continue my spawning survey alone. We were both enjoying our newfound ability to pursue frivolous and quixotic projects together, but the press of work and responsibility too often cut them short.

Cottonwood was the next creek, and it ran right through the middle of Nelson. After passing underneath a highway cloverleaf worthy of Los Angeles, the creek flows through the petroleum-soaked CPR railyards, passes alongside the school district's bus yard, and then empties into the West Arm just downstream from the airport and the municipal garbage transfer station. Cottonwood's delta is quite large, providing much of the ground that the city's lower downtown is built on. The bottom part of the creek, from the CPR yards down to the mouth, is riprapped with broken concrete along both banks, but some years back a local fish and wildlife group built three lovely spawning beds, laying down crushed gravel and separating each with log deadheads stretched right across the stream. In spite of the habitat restoration effort, there were no fish here either. The gravel looked suspiciously silty and algae-coated. I wondered if the beds had ever been used at all. In the CPR yards, the Cottonwood was channelled into a series of fish-hostile concrete flumes. Above the yards, and within the crushing embrace of the cloverleaf, the creek is actually allowed a contradictory bit of wildness. Alongside its tangled banks sits a Nelson institution, the farmer's market, which has little to do with agriculture and is a kind of weekend experiment in Third World living. Above the market is the once-lovely Cottonwood Falls, a definite showstopper for spawning even if there were no more concrete flumes above it, which there are. During my walk from the Cottonwood's mouth to the falls I drew many suspicious looks, but never saw a single kokanee. Anderson Creek was a write-off; a few metres from the mouth it entered a darkened culvert of unknown length.

I spotted a single fish and hoped an appropriate mate would join it soon, before it gave itself over to the ospreys.

As I surveyed further, moving upstream toward the main lake, Five Mile Creek came next. The mouth of Five Mile forms a smaller delta known as Troup Junction, where the now-abandoned Burlington Northern rail lines used to join the CPR mainline. Five Mile is like Grohman, a small, high-gradient or steeply sloping stream, but the area around the mouth does contain a few snags, pools, and small gravels. I spotted a single fish and hoped an appropriate mate would join it soon, before it gave itself over to the ospreys.

I skipped the next creeks, Duhamel and Sitkum, because both had been riprapped and channelled into residential submission. Next was Lasca, a larger stream with a broad delta. The delta is called Yaksakukeni, Place of Many Redfish, by the Sinixt. Generations of that nation's experience and observation lie buried amongst the scrub willows and sweetgrass along the creek. European settlers retitled it Atbara, the name of a tributary of the Nile River. The origin of the name Lasca is a mystery. Some local residents claim it comes from a board game of the same name, invented by chess champion Emanuel Lasker in 1911. Others point to the 1919 silent western movie *Lasca*, starring Frank May and Edith Roberts. Lasca and Atbara are typical settler place names of the Kootenays. Existing indigenous place names were largely ignored, and references to British Empire and American places abound. It is refreshing to run across the occasional place name that reflects a kind of earthy settler indigeny, like Giveout or 49 Creek.

Old-timers remember boating to the mouth of Lasca in the fall to fork spent kokanee carcasses into barrels, to be used to fertilize the gardens of Nelson. But after years of streambed modification, nutrient depletion, dam-induced water fluctuations, and the disastrous Mysis shrimp introduction, the Lasca spawning population had collapsed. By the early 1990s it was down to less than a hundred spawners, but word was that the recent lake fertilization project had caused the numbers to rebound. Lasca did not share the same history of massive disturbance that Cottonwood did, but I had no doubt it had been modified in some way, whether by mining, water diversion, or the railroad.

Trudging down the beach toward the mouth of Lasca, I notice the sumac bushes, their leaves bright red with fall colour. This colour change, from ordinary green to kokanee red, was celebrated as a seasonal marker by the local Sinixt, a biological signpost announcing the kokanee spawning season and the fishing associated with it. Farther down the beach I see a dead spawner, its head case already picked open by seagulls. Skeptically, I think it could have washed over here from the Fish and Wildlife spawning beds at nearby Kokanee Creek, the primary spawning ground of the West Arm population.

The mouth of Lasca is choked with tangled willow and dogwood, so I force my way slowly through thickets, peering at the water when I can. Reaching a riffle, I pull the branches aside and am delighted to see seven brightly coloured fish. The pool at the head of the riffle contains twenty more. By the time I reach a second deep pool, my count is over fifty. I stand a long time, watching the fish as they pulse. One suddenly takes off on a diagonal run, and the others react by starting runs of their own, scattering the school like so many billiard balls. The slightly larger male fish, who have a pronounced dorsal hump and sport overshot lower jaws, are responsible for most of the constant alarms and excursions. They fiercely defend a chosen territory one moment, then abandon it the next.

In amongst the normal-sized fish I see what fisheries biologist Ken Ashley calls "the sneakers," very small males, only two years old, hoping for some action. Ashley thinks the sneakers provide a kind of species safety net. If something happens to the full-grown three- and four-year-old males — disease, landslides, a period of adverse weather — the sneakers may ensure that some fertilization does occur.

Lasca's water is transparent, but like window glass turned on edge it has a wonderful liquid green cast to it. The reds of the kokanee range from copper through goldfish, fire engine, and burnt sienna to the bleached pink of the dead. The streambed below the fish forms an elegant background of rounded stones of various colours. A single cottonwood leaf, unexpected messenger of fall, spirals down to land gently and precisely in the centre of the pool. This, I muse, must be what the Japanese strive to create in their water gardens, a kind of elevated harmony and restfulness based on careful composition. Elements of rock, water, and vegetation are placed just so, and then the placement is validated

Each new pool contains more kokanee, and at something like 250, I give up my count, reassured.

by the introduction of fish that are bred to be living works of art. My head begins to spin as I try to decide whether nature is imitating art or art nature, or if perhaps there is no meaningful boundary between the two.

The creek climbs gradually as I explore further. Dense willows give way to more open cedar, and I no longer have to thrash my way along. Each new pool contains more kokanee, and at something like 250, I give up my count, reassured. Lasca is on the road to recovery. One deep pool contains a couple of real hook-jawed lunkers, probably weighing seven or eight pounds, successful scions of a thousand Lasca generations. Kootenay rock and Kootenay water have fused to produce this exotic organism. Now, after an epoch of wilful ignorance followed by one of humble apprenticeship, we settlers have a small role in mediating that fusion.

Spawning habitat is not the limiting factor for the kokanee in this lake; food is. The whole Lasca run could probably be eliminated without jeopardizing the overall lake population. But there is a kind of rightness to Lasca, to a species reclaiming a piece of its own habitat, however insignificant that piece may be. The fact that we have a hand in restoring that population and its habitat allows us to put our previous callousness into perspective. I feel a kind of modest regional patriotism, here on the tangled banks of Lasca Creek. People of this region have moved from colonial indifference through industrial devastation to, finally, an actual relationship with these fish.

Rounding Lasca's next bend, I am confronted by an imposing concrete railroad bridge. This is the Lasca Creek flume, a short and massive tunnel of concrete, with equally massive abutments on either side. Numbers nearly obliterated by moss proudly announce the date "1908" to the assembled cedars upstream. In the bottom of the flume lies another huge slab of concrete, reinforced with old railway tracks. Water hurtles over the six metres of smooth concrete surface and then spills violently into the plunge pool below the flume. Burst speed again: physiological limitations. I know immediately that the creation of this concrete flume slammed the door on any spawning upstream of it. I cross the tracks and continue upstream along the creek for some distance, just to confirm my suspicions. There are no fish. Further on, a recent clearcut begins just a few metres from the creekbed. Rounding another bend I come on a rotting, half-buried rock crib, probably from some hundred-year-old gold-sluicing operation.

Lasca's sandy delta forms a convex semicircle that extends out into the West Arm. Lakeward beyond the delta is a shoal, marked with a navigational light on the top of a piling. Like many pilings up and down the West Arm, it hosts an osprey nest. As I climb into the boat for the return trip to Nelson, the owner of the nest passes low overhead, clutching a heavy spawner in its talons. The spawner wriggles and thrashes about, causing momentary interruptions of the osprey's determined flight from the creek mouth back to the piling. Once the bird reaches the piling, it has to circle it several times to reach the nest, as a heavily loaded airplane might spiral upward to reach cruising altitude.

The osprey is fitted precisely to the kokanee. It cruises and hovers high above the clear waters of the lake and the West Arm, watching for an unsuspecting fish to come to the surface. Its silent, crumpled plunge is followed by a last-second opening of wings and inversion of the body; talons extend at splashdown, clench firmly onto the back of the fish, and suddenly this graceful bird turns into a beast of burden as its powerful wingbeats lift it off the surface of the water. The whole event, from the beginning of the dive to the capture, happens in a heartbeat.

This osprey and its fledglings will leave the piling shortly, headed south on a twenty- to thirty-day migration flight to wintering grounds in Mexico. Their departure will be timed to coincide with the end of the spawning season, so they have had a full month of bulking up on the easily available fat and protein provided by the spawners.

Lasca Creek, then, is linked northward to the Aleutian Islands, where the sockeye progenitors of the kokanee feed, and southward to Tampico, where the kokanee-fuelled osprey will winter. As I learn these ecological linkages, I begin to see how they spin outward, anastomose, and densify across the known landscape. Making my way slowly home down the West Arm, ever mindful of the propeller, I am pleased to know that my little region is carefully held in a larger matrix of sinuous biological threads that reach to Mexico and Alaska.

Sport fishing for kokanee on the West Arm of Kootenay Lake in May 1999. The best time to fish is early in the morning, when the kokanee are feeding near the surface. PHOTO BY ART STOCK

Fishing

Red Wassick is a fisherman born. As a kid living in Nelson in the 1930s, he developed an elaborate Depression-era technology for catching kokanee. His pole was a dried cane from an elderberry bush. Line was a thick linen variety known as cutty hunk. The leader was catgut, which had to be carefully soaked before it could be used, and a bent fence staple served as the hook. Maggots foraged from roadkill were used for bait. In the fall, Red would get up early, before school, to fish at the Nelson ferry dock. On his way down, he would collect a handful of spilled oats from the West Transfer Company horse stables and then join his fishing colleagues at the dock. It was an odd grouping, these half dozen Chinese men and ten-year-old Red, but they were a fraternity and learned from each other. Before casting his line, Red would throw out the oats as chum, to attract fish.

Sixty years later, Red still goes out every morning early. His gear has changed radically, and now he ranges up and down the length of the West Arm in his boat, but his original fascination with fish and fishing remains intact.

As the dean of West Arm fishers, Red is often consulted by scientists and biologists working on the kokanee. Because of the fragility of the population, Ministry of Environment biologists keep close tabs on the fish; season openings and closings vary from year to year and can change with as little as one day's notice.

Before the spring season opens, the biologists often ask Red to do a "test fish" to see how many he will catch in an hour, and they adjust the season length based on his results.

The primary challenge for the kokanee angler is to get his gear down deep, where the fish spend a lot of their time. Using large weights or weighted line means that you have very little sense of playing the small kokanee, so some fishermen use a downrigger arrangement, which carries a lightly weighted line down to the right depth and then releases it.

The next question is how deep to fish. Kokanee and other fish like to hang along the thermocline, a layer of productive water sandwiched between the warm surface layer and the cold layer underneath. That thermocline varies with season and location, so sonar fish finders are common accessories on kokanee fishers' boats. As fish writer Dave Biser says, what starts out as a plain rowboat often becomes encrusted with more gadgets than a Japanese fishing trawler.

Dave Biser, KOKANEE: A COMPLETE FISHING GUIDE *(Portland, OR: Frank Amato Publications, 1998).*

The alternative to going down deep is to get up very early in the morning, when the kokanee are feeding near the surface. Red and many other fishermen prefer this time, before the rest of the world is up and morning traffic begins rumbling down Highway 3A.

Lures for kokanee are generally of the flashy, hardware kind. No one has ever been able to explain to me why a fish addicted to microscopic copepods would bite on a brightly coloured slab of tin, but they do. Red's neatly organized tackle boxes contain Deadly Dick lures of various weights. He likes to "sweeten" his lures by applying reflective strips to them, and then he jigs the lure in a certain way, with a wrist action refined over seven decades.

Kokanee can be caught on dry flies in the summer. Devotees of the gentle art of fly fishing must have a light hand, though, since the kokanee has a small, soft mouth and will immediately throw the hook if played roughly.

Over time there have been two different fishing cultures on Kootenay Lake. The Aboriginal one was communal, based on subsistence, and focussed around major falls, like Bonnington, and major spawning runs, like Lasca. The British fishing tradition that came with European settlement was far different, being individual, dispersed, and largely recreational. Fishing and hunting, in the eyes of the early promoters of settlement in the Kootenays, was an integral component of the ozonated and manly lifestyle of the Kootenay yeoman who owned his plot of ground, farmed it with his wife and kids, and brought lots of fish and game home for dinner. Early books written by European adventurers in the Kootenays, such as Baillie-Grohman, Lees and Clutterbuck, Hornaday, and Bealby, laid the groundwork for the area's fishing and hunting mystique, which was further enhanced by a whole series of bad regional travel books. Immigrants from the British Isles, many of them inspired by this literature, began arriving in the Kootenays in large numbers by the early 1900s.

A couple of samples, first from Lees and Clutterbuck: "The light of the setting sun glowing on those wonderful red-barked trees, making more glorious by the contrast with their long dark shadows the brilliantly lighted glades of yellow grass, and tinting with the same ruddy hue the foliage which half concealed their stately pillars, its delicate needles already turning into gold under the Midas-touch of King Frost."

And from Evah McKowan: "My own personal sunbeams are, at this moment, stealthily climbing up behind the Canyon hill. Then, all of a sudden, they are over on the top of Goat Mountain, crowning it with opal and dispelling its white-cloud nightcap. This done, they move joyfully down to spend the day with me."

With the success of the fertilization project, both the kokanee and the rainbow are back on a reduced but stable footing. Fishing culture is now free to develop again, but as a highly controlled and fragile exercise. Current fishing expectations are far lower than those of the early Kootenay yeoman, but we accept these incremental declines so long as the rituals of fishing are preserved. One of the most important of those rituals is that of fathers and sons. As a kind of neutral ground, fishing has defused the inevitable tension from generations of father-son relationships, including mine.

Some of those lurid regional travel books are: Mrs. Algernon St. Maur's IMPRESSIONS OF A TENDERFOOT *(London: John Murray Publishers, 1890), R.E. Vernede's* THE FAIR DOMINION *(Toronto: Wm. Briggs Publishers, 1911), Walter Dwight Wilcox's* CAMPING IN THE CANADIAN ROCKIES *(New York: Knickerbocker Press, 1896), Evah McKowan's* JANET OF KOOTENAY *(New York: G.H. Doran and Co., 1919), J.A. Lees & W.J. Clutterbuck's* BC 1887: A RAMBLE IN BRITISH COLUMBIA *(London: Longmans, Green & Co., 1889), and W.A. Baillie-Grohman's* FIFTEEN YEARS' SPORT AND LIFE IN THE HUNTING GROUNDS OF WESTERN AMERICA AND BRITISH COLUMBIA *(London: Horace Cox, 1900).*

A kokanee after spawning. Like the autumn leaves, the kokanee's colour ranges from copper to fire-engine red. PHOTO BY ART STOCK.

Bioregion

September. Whole families line the spawning channel at Kokanee Creek Park, staring down at the seething mass of red backs, sometimes for hours. The season is changing, the new school year has started, and the park's summer playground aspect is giving way to the sombre, workaday look of fall. Brisk air is filled with new beginnings and wood smoke. The summer tourists are all gone, and local families are here to take a last wistful look at the swimming beach, stand close to the barbecue, and watch the fish.

The spawning channel is a kind of long amphitheatre, with massive old cottonwoods towering overhead. The natural stream channel has been blocked off by a fish weir, and the ascending spawners are re-routed to this special side channel, which has been carefully and hopefully re-engineered to kokanee specifications, with long, straight, stairstepped beds of meticulously selected gravel, covered by water of precise depth and speed. A broad, wheelchair-accessible walkway that can accommodate six abreast follows the channel, and a wooden railing separates the two. The railing is just right to lean against, and people do, adults against the top rail, kids against the lower one, mesmerized. Watching.

The kokanee spawners have navigated back to their natal stream by a combination of water chemistry and magic, a far lesser feat than the 2000-kilometre returns of their cousins the sockeye, but still remarkable. By now the fish have turned from burnished silver to a lurid combination of fire-engine red and frog green, as if to advertise their promiscuity, their protein, their imminent death.

I watch too, knowing that beyond their elegant and complex biology, these fish hold a deeper meaning for us, a meaning both personal and communal at the same time. But the seething red backs form a complex hieroglyphic, whose meanings are not easily deciphered. We locals do have a natural bond with this creature, because we both share a unique piece of geography. The human construct we call the Kootenays overlaps nicely with the kokanee's natural range. Although the fish is found widely in lakes along the North Pacific littoral, this lake, and this folded region of rock and water, is kokanee heartland. What we participate in, the kokanee does too, often to its detriment. And what it participates in, from proglacial lakes to the taste of Daphnia and the feel of the thermocline, also has meaning for me. The kokanee speaks from that distant and eroded time when the animal world held both literal and symbolic meaning for the human world. As red backs knife through the water, the crisp September air settles slowly toward winter, and a foraging ouzel works the rocks at the edge of the spawning channel, we can privately acknowledge that these animals still hold symbolic meanings. As I learn about the kokanee, somehow I am better able to understand the cycle of life, the meaning of family, the pull of home.

This pilot fish is also leading me forward, past mere biology and ecology, into an unexpected Kootenay bioregionalism. The kokanee is the symbol, the fundamental ur-creature of this region, the totem. Totem is part of what we yearn for, as we lean on those September railings. But no matter how hard we try, we cannot make totems, and we cannot create bioregions, from science alone. The vast amount of information that science has generated about the Kootenays has not moved us one millimetre closer to bonding with this accordion-folded country, but science together with art, respect for First Nations knowledge, and especially the creation of new mythologies of our own can move us forward into a dynamic empathy with the regional landscape.

How do you create such a regional mythology? You might start in midsummer, on the water, far enough upstream from Nelson so you can just see the distant Purcell Mountains through the narrow gunsight of the West Arm. Paddle a kayak or canoe over to the unpopulated south shore. Seen now from water level, the surrounding mountains capture and reflect more light, and the moment turns serene. Even in July, cottonwood fluff still floats on the air, uncertain of its direction. Clothed in cedar and Douglas-fir, the mountains come precipitously down to the water and then plunge right in, continuing downward below the water surface. As you glide closer to the south shore, the solid green of forest cover opens to expose slabs of grey-black granite, partly scabbed over with lush green moss. The steep plunge of mountain toward the lake is interrupted only by a spidery rail line blasted into rock just above the water. Contemplate the history and impacts the railroad has had on our region. Tie up to a snag, and step out onto a flat rock that rests a few inches below the water surface. From there, slide slowly into water that looks and feels like cold green champagne. You may use the artifact of a mask and wetsuit to do so, as you are merely a guest here anyway. Observe the jumbled rocks beneath you. Some are glacier-rounded, others freshly broken and sharp, and all naked except for the faintest suggestion of algae film. The rock field continues steeply down toward green oblivion, to where sunlight disappears completely, about thirty metres below. Welcome to a silent universe composed of water, rock, and sunlight, with tenuous strands of biology in between; welcome to pure Kootenay oligotrophy. If you stay long enough, a sucker fish will pass mildly underneath you, and perhaps the shadow of an observant osprey overhead. Would you see a kokanee? Only if you were very lucky.

The regional mythology you create may be spoken, written, woven, carved, thrown, filmed, or painted; there are no prescriptions for its medium. The only requirement is passionate immersion in the local. Your mythology's impact should diminish when it is appreciated outside of its own native region, but only slightly, since the local, when passionately observed and keenly wrought, is universal.

Bioregionalism built on regional mythology is a messy, contradictory, and dangerous idea. Of bioregionalism's many definitions, perhaps the most obvious is a collective attention to — and sense of — place. Bioregionalism is the transformation of our lives by local biology, geology, climate. As the poet Gary Snyder says, the strength of the bond to place is second only to the bond of kinship. Bioregionalism at its root is instinct, one that has probably been with us since we walked upright. In the development of the human, there was a long stage in which intimate knowledge of one's home landscape was a powerful adaptive advantage. That knowledge may become adaptive again, in this new era of human evolution, where our fight is for sanity and integrity, rather than for mere survival.

Bioregionalism is the transformation of our lives by local biology, geology, climate.

Our longstanding instinct for bioregionalism was only recently defined as a philosophy, when writers and activists like Peter Berg, Freeman House, Gary Snyder, and British Columbia's own Doug Aberley, Terry Glavin, Chris and Judith Plant, and others shaped it into a formal notion. Inherent in bioregionalism is the idea that places are unique and distinct, and that people are changed — uniquely and distinctly — by living in those particular places. Cheap energy, which means that the carrots we eat are grown in Mexico instead of Creston, and pervasive television, which means we passively accept entertainment created in New York instead of actively seeking it out in Cranbrook or Salmo, are massive deterrents to developing bioregionalism.

We have a local beer, brewed in Creston, called Kokanee. Clever television ad campaigns show brown bottles fighting their way upstream and doing salmonid-like jumps in white water. When the voice-over declares "Kokanee, it's the beer out here," it mouths a confused but powerful sentiment, the desire for regional differences. The desire to belong, to a unique landscape and to a particular human community. Even when diverted into the shallows of product advertising, the simple phrase "out here" hints of a conscious loyalty to place and to a particular place-influenced way of doing things. It is not surprising that the brewery chose the kokanee as the name for its beer. Advertisers fully understand the power of symbol.

Ordinary people may be less analytical about symbols, but

they still feel their power. The Ministry of Water, Land and Air Protection monitors the numbers of juvenile kokanee fry every spring. The fry leave the creeks and head for the West Arm under cover of darkness, when they have the best chance to avoid the many predators that await them. The biggest movement of fry occurs on rainy, windy, and moonless nights. My wife and I accompanied Gary, a ministry fisheries technician, on such a night. We watched as he dipped his nets into Kokanee Creek and then quickly counted the gasping, writhing fry. Up close, under the light of a headlamp, they were tiny slivers of moonlight with huge and accusing eyes. The counts would go on all night on a precise schedule: dip, count, quickly throw back, wait, dip again. Gary, the technician, said to us, "You know, I've never felt smaller or more alone than at three in the morning in the dark and the pouring rain, holding a handful of kokanee fry."

I think I understand what Gary meant. In his hand he held complex, squirming fragments of an entire ecosystem, one that had nothing to do with him. We humans are the interlopers here: we are like the lonely and self-conscious teenager on the awkward first day at a new school, looking enviously at the established relationships, the camaraderie, the self-sufficiency of nature. No part of this ecosystem needs us to function. This sense of insignificance in the face of a complete, self-sufficient nature is a new and healthy sentiment. It rests uneasily with a more traditional concept, that the fry are completely dependent on our intervention, and a completely new one, that we and the kokanee are destined to work out a relationship of equals.

We are beginning to practise an ecology of inclusion. First we ignored ecology altogether. Then we began to study it species by species — population dynamics, reproductive biology, and so on. Now we study the species together with its habitat, and some have gone even further and proposed that if the entire habitat is in order, the species pretty well look after themselves. The next natural step in the hierarchy of inclusive ecology is to bring the messy, unpredictable, and problematic human into it.

The habitat of the human, its event field, the extent of the landscape that affects people and is affected by people, is another definition of a bioregion.

Bioregionalism is subversive because it is neither politics nor ideology. Therefore it is incomprehensible to those in power. It is anarchic, and totally outside of official sanction. In fact, our current economy drives us toward precisely the opposite premise; we are supposed to converge around a single, worldwide commercial culture, where goods and services are harmonized to eliminate local variation. Labour, capital, and products are predestined to settle into a seamless flow from one anonymous market area to another, reacting only to supply, demand, and profit. Bioregionalism would subvert all this, bypassing many globally mass-marketed cultural products, in favour of the local. Together with the recognition of the unique biophysical features of a region, bioregionalism should also recognize and encourage what is unique and distinct about the human culture of the region. And in order to be successful, biocultural regionalism must come to terms with both First Nations and settler culture elements.

Spokane or the Okanagan is half a day away, but other than for the rare weekend shopping trip, these locations might as well be on another planet.

Bioregionalism is not only subversive; it is also marginal. The more isolated an area is, the further it is from the cultural mainstream, the less clout it has on the provincial or national scene, the more likely it is to have some elements of bioregionalism already, and the more likely it is to further develop those elements. As Terry Glavin says, the people of the twenty-five or so distinct eco-regions of British Columbia are positioned, perhaps better than anywhere else in North America, to recast some of these fundamental issues of place, social relation, and sustainability in the form of new bioregional cultures.

In the Kootenays, I see the ideal location for a bioregional culture. Who are we Kootenaians? Well, we are a full day's drive from either Calgary or Vancouver. Although we do travel to those places on occasion, we are completely out of their orbit. Spokane or the Okanagan is half a day away, but other than for the rare weekend shopping trip, these locations might as well be on another planet. The two local airports, Cranbrook and Castlegar, offer only expensive, unreliable connector flights into the main east-west routes. Castlegar airport's famous winter valley cloud and challenging approach have earned it the nickname "Cancel-gar." Like the kokanee, we are cut off. Those long drives and low winter cloud ceilings and mountain passes are our Bonnington Falls. Like the kokanee, we adjust to our isolation. Then, at a certain point, we look back and realize that relative isolation, and relative intimacy with the terms of our geography, have changed us, as they changed the kokanee, and we are pleased with our transformation. There is a bashful, self-deprecating, but persistent pride about living here, about being local.

People who lead tightly scheduled lives, who depend on cell phones and shuttle between commitments in major cities, simply cannot live in the Kootenays. The pace of life here is a little slower, a little more rooted. More than once I have had the experience of walking down Nelson's Baker Street, preoccupied with some nameless urgency, only to realize I was walking too fast and subtly disrupting the relaxed flow of pedestrians around me. In Nelson, walking at Vancouver speed is simply inappropriate.

As a bioregion, we must also deal with local complexity and local differences. Early on, "Kootenay" split into "the Kootenays," acknowledging two distinct cultures and ecologies. The Purcell Mountains divide our region into East Kootenay and West Kootenay. The East Kootenays, basically the broad valley of the Rocky Mountain Trench, has a definite prairie energy, with a partly continental climate of warm summers and relatively dry, cold winters. Fifteen mountain passes through the Rockies have resulted in a strong prairie influence in the trench. The eastbound traveller on Highway 3 first sees the broad trench and the Rockies through a notch in the valley east of Moyie. Mount Fisher looms, its jagged shape chiselled across the sky, a classic Rockies mountain. In winter it often hosts its own lenticular cloud, curved over the summit.

Coming back to Nelson — in the heart of the West Kootenays — one returns to a totally different world of dense forest and dark rock. Rags of lingering cloud are caught and held on windless mountainsides. The West Kootenays are known ecologically as a "coastal refugium," where rain, heavy snowfall, and mild winters allow plants like salal, devil's club, and western red cedar to grow, hundreds of kilometres away from their centre of abundance on the coast. There is even a disjunct pocket of yellow cedar thriving in the Slocan Valley, a species that belongs along the fogbound shores of the North Pacific. Botanists assume that these coastal species are a legacy of an earlier, more maritime climate that allowed them to spread right across the province, and the West Kootenays is the last remaining pocket of maritime-influenced Interior vegetation.

Mixed together with the coastal refugees, often on the same mountainside, are sentinels of the dry Interior — ponderosa pine, rough fescue, and alligator lizards. The Kootenays are a complex ecological tangle, as well as a human one.

There is a fundamental social split between the East and West Kootenays. If I needed to buy a hunting knife, or hip-waders, I would certainly shop for them in Cranbrook. If a hackeysack or a handmade hat were on my list, I would look for them in Nelson. But the situation is actually much more complicated than that. Communities of the Kootenays range from industrial to New Age and back again; downtown Trail is built around a massive lead–zinc smelter, while Rossland, ten kilometres away, is caught up with crystals, cappuccinos, and snowboards. New Denver celebrates environmentalism; adjacent Nakusp seems to be the last refuge of clearcut logging. Spread-out Castlegar welcomes strip malls and fast-food franchises; compact Nelson is a downtown-oriented, owner-operated kind of place. Invermere is heavily influenced by Calgary; Cranbrook is nobody's suburb. Sparwood and the coal communities of the Elk Valley are another universe apart. Trail, Rossland, and Fernie all share a common heritage of radical labour movements, dormant now but perhaps someday to resurrect themselves in a new form.

Ethnic and lifestyle complexity further complicates the two Kootenays and binds them together. Swiss mountain guides, Quebecois treeplanters, German foresters, third-generation Italian immigrants, American draft-dodgers, nomadic skiers, dreadlocked hippies, suspendered loggers, Vancouver refugees, Ktunaxa, Shuswap, and Sinixt, descendants of Second World War Japanese internees, lesbian farmers, California telecommuters, nouveau Buddhists, and back-to-the-land dreamers from every jurisdiction help create the human fabric of the region. East and West Kootenay engage radically different ecologies and sensibilities, yet I know of a hundred intimate linkages — hydrographic, historic, jurisdictional, personal — that bind them together. The kokanee forms one of those links.

The boundary between Pacific and Mountain Time Zones wanders down the spine of the Purcells, splitting the East and West Kootenays into two time zones, except for Creston, which marches to West Kootenay time in the summer and East Kootenay time in the winter. Missed appointments and meetings are common.

A Kootenay bioregionalism needs to be felt at gut level. The spawning habits of local fish, the feel of your own town on a Friday afternoon as people gear down for the weekend, the geological history of local landforms, all must be experienced and internalized. Some years ago the *Whole Earth Review* magazine proposed a now-famous bioregional quiz, which asked questions like "Name the waterbody that your domestic water comes from" and "Name two native bird species that nest in your area." The quiz seemed artificial, but it drove home the point that many of us didn't know that kind of basic information and had never even thought about it.

> *If I needed to buy a hunting knife, or hip-waders, I would certainly shop for them in Cranbrook. If a hackeysack or a handmade hat were on my list, I would look for them in Nelson.*

We definitely have the raw materials for a brash, earthy, and innovative Kootenay bioregional culture, plus the human energy and diversity to build it. The Kootenay-Boundary Land Use Plan, an outgrowth of the provincial Commission on Resources and the Environment (CORE) process, released some of that energy and set the stage for an attempt at bioregionalism. The Land Use planning process brought together all the economic, environmental, and recreational sectors to work out zones of influence and reduce resource conflicts on Crown land, which makes up the vast majority of the Kootenay landbase. The sectoral representation around the planning table was daunting. Foresters, miners, ranchers, and guide-outfitters worked out details with parks advocates, environmentalists, small business people, fishers, and trappers. Going well beyond the usual B.C. stalemate of loggers with their jobs versus environmentalists with their old growth, the process produced a number of minor revelations and unexpected points of agreement. When they finished in 1998, the scarred veterans of the plan round-table had achieved a surprising degree of consensus and were prepared to soldier on with their innovative work. Officials were stunned by this unprecedented accord, so the Kootenay-Boundary Land Use Plan was hastily buttoned up and shuffled inside the safer confines of the government ministries.

As a minor participant in the Land Use Plan exercise, I marvelled at the process, the number of sectors represented, and the level of commitment, but I always left the meetings with a nagging feeling that something was missing. Finally, it dawned on me; there were no storytellers in attendance. No poets. No oral historians, no balladeers.

Storytelling and the oral tradition are crucial to the development and maintenance of a place mythology, but that tradition is weak in the settler cultures of western Canada, and what little tradition exists is continuously eroded by mass media culture. If we are to actually create a local narrative tradition, there are few precedents to build on. We are spoon-fed a mass culture that is suspicious of both narrative and of place, and we turn increasingly to that haven of atomistic, placeless particularity, the internet. It is no wonder that broad-based regional stories are few and far between.

As one small initiative in the development of bioregional and storytelling culture, I suggest the use of successional pathways and food chains. This information is not "owned" by any particular group, and it has good narrative and rhythmic potential. A written version of one branch of the kokanee food chain might go something like this:

> dissolved phosphorous to floating diatom, harvester of
>   Kootenay sunlight
> from diatom to tiny invertebrate Daphnia
> from Daphnia to silvery kokanee, molten essence of
>   our landscape
> from spawned-out fall kokanee to hibernation-
>   minded black bear

phosphorous from bear scat captured by Douglas
   maple leaf
leaf falls, flows down steep and cedar-bounded creek
   to Kootenay Lake
elusive phosphorous captured again by diatom

This tale could be woven, expanded, and told in different ways, with different media. The fact that our knowledge of food chains is incomplete, and our knowledge of successional pathways even more so, would be a creative asset to this new phase of regional culture-building, encouraging us to speculate, research, and reinterpret.

I hope our kokanee prosper. As I glimpse the molten silver fry coming down the creeks on rainy and moonless spring nights, or marvel at the fiery red spawners returning on the quickening days of fall, I know these fish are a part of me, a clean and dignified and rooted part. I am glad that our futures are so entangled.

Bibliography

Ashley, Ken, et al. "Restoration of an Interior Lake System: The Kootenay Lake Fertilization Experiment." *Water Quality Res. J. Canada* 32, no. 2 (1997): 295-323.

Biser, Dave. *Kokanee: A Complete Fishing Guide*. Portland, OR: Frank Amato Publications, 1998.

Bouchard, Randy, et al. *Lakes, Okanagan and Shuswap Knowledge and Use of the Keenleyside Powerplant Project Study Area*. Victoria: Columbia Power Corp, 1998.

Columbia Basin Fish & Wildlife Compensation Program. Program Updates and Project Handbooks. Nelson, BC: CBFWC.

Daley, R.J., et al. *Effects of Upstream Impoundments on the Limnology of Kootenay Lake, BC*. Scientific Series 117. Vancouver: National Water Research Institute, 1981.

Dawson, George M. "Notes on the Shuswap People of British Columbia." In *Transactions of the Royal Society of Canada*, Section II, Part 1, pp. 3-44. Royal Society of Canada, 1891.

Haig-Brown, Roderick. *The Western Angler*. New York: Wm. Morrow & Co., 1947.

Harden, Blaine. *A River Lost: The Life and Death of the Columbia*. New York: Norton and Co., 1996.

Lichatowich, Jim. *Salmon Without Rivers*. Covelo, CA: Island Press, 1999.

Martin, A.D. and T.G. Northcote. "Kootenay Lake: An Inappropriate Model for *Mysis relicta* Introduction into North Temperate Lakes." *American Fisheries Society Symposium* 9 (1991): 23-29.

Northcote, T.G. *Some Impacts of Man on Kootenay Lake and its Salmonids*. Technical Report. 25. Ann Arbor, MI: Great Lakes Fishery Commission, 1973.

Quammen, David. "A Planet of Weeds." *Harpers Magazine* (October
    1998): pp. 57-69.
Rhenisch, Harold. *Tom Thomson's Shack*. Vancouver: New Star Books,
    2000.
Scott, W.B. and E.J. Crossman. *Freshwater fishes of Canada*. Bulletin
    184. Fisheries Research Board of Canada, 1973.
Wood, Tom. "The Larkin Legacy: Fisheries Management in BC." *BC
    Outdoors* (March 1989).

TRANSMONTANUS is edited by Terry Glavin. Editorial correspondence should be sent to Transmontanus, PO Box C25, Fernhill Road, Mayne Island, BC V0N 2J0.

New Star Books Ltd.
107 - 3477 Commercial Street
Vancouver, BC
V5N 4E8
www.NewStarBooks.com
info@NewStarBooks.com

Edited for press by Audrey McClellan
Cover by Rayola Graphic Design
Cover photo by Art Stock
Maps by Eric Leinberger
Typesetting by New Star Books
Printed & bound in Canada by AGMV-Marquis Imprimeur
First printing September 2002

Publication of this work is made possible by grants from the Canada Council, the British Columbia Arts Council, and the Department of Canadian Heritage Book Publishing Industry Development Program.

NATIONAL LIBRARY OF CANADA CATALOGUING IN PUBLICATION DATA

Gayton, Don, 1946–
 Kokanee

(Transmontanus, ISSN 1200-3336; v. 9)
Includes bibliographical references.
ISBN 0-921586-85-x

1. Kokanee salmon — Habitat — British Columbia — Kootenay Region.   I. Title.   II. Series.
QL638.S2G39 2002   597.5'6   C2002-910827-6

AGMV Marquis

MEMBER OF SCABRINI MEDIA

Quebec, Canada
2002